BEYOND CODE

Learn to distinguish yourself in 9 simple steps!

With warm wishes,
Rajesh
April 2007.

ADVANCE PRAISE

Thought Leaders and Authors

This book is filled with solid advice and timeless wisdom for anyone dealing with the pressures of doing business in a 24/7 world.

Bo Burlingham, Editor at Large, Inc. Magazine,
Co-author of *The Great Game of Business*

Beyond Code is packed with wisdom. It should be required reading for every young professional, and remedial reading for many further along in their careers.

David Maister, Author and Consultant

Beyond Code is a little powerhouse of a book—an explosive mix of inspiration and instruction, exercises and enthusiasm. Every software professional will benefit from reading it and absorbing its wisdom.

Daniel H. Pink, Author of *Free Agent Nation* and
A Whole New Mind

Rajesh has captured the essence of what makes a true professional in any industry. A true professional—a great consultant—is someone who is a great person, and Rajesh explains just how you can go from good to great consultant in this slim, engaging book. "

Dave Taylor, Strategic Management Consultant,
Intuitive Systems, Inc.

Rajesh has written the best book yet for IT pros who wish to distinguish themselves, and have a good time in the process.

Doc Searls, Author, "The Cluetrain Manifesto," and
Senior Editor, Linux Journal

A quick guide to things every geek should understand.
Guy Kawasaki, Author of *The Art of the Start*

Witty, creative, succinct, insightful! This little book is ideal for anyone with a big dream.

Marcia Wieder, America's Dream Coach

Beyond Code is not just great for software consultants—it is great for ALL consultants!

Marshall Goldsmith, Author of *The Leader of the Future* and *The Art and Practice of Leadership Coaching*.

A true masterpiece that magnificently blends solid practical advice with inspiration and enlightenment. **Beyond Code** will reignite your passion and show you the clear path to create a successful career.

Peggy McColl, Author of *The 8 Proven Secrets to SMART Success*

Whether you are a novice or a seasoned veteran, you will discover golden nuggets that will help you with personal and business growth.

Stephen M. Shapiro, Author of *24/7 Innovation*, and the soon-to-be-released book, *Goal-Free Living*

Rajesh understands what makes the biggest difference in project and technology management—*people*. This book will give any reader a tool kit to avoid "thing thinking" and manage way beyond simple code. If you want to retain top talent and bring out their best, this book is for you. If you want to make a difference to your business and the people that comprise it, this book is for you. Read it and grow.

Tim Sanders, Author of *Love is the Killer App: How to win business and influence friends* and Leadership Coach at Yahoo!

Software & Services Leaders

Remarkable service organizations are built by remarkable people.

If you want your people to be remarkable, hand them a copy of **Beyond Code**.

> **Arjun Malhotra,** Chairman and CEO, Headstrong Inc.

Rajesh Setty has explained seemingly complex issues using the simplest of words and examples. **Beyond Code** is a must-read for today's IT consultants, especially those who have recently embarked on this exciting career path.

> **Jerry Rao,** Chairman & CEO, Mphasis BFL Limited

While using a simple, and easy to understand style, Rajesh has done a super job to give the readers powerful and practical suggestions to improve their effectiveness. For practicing consultants and professionals the book provides an excellent refresher course and a handy guide for future assignments. Young professionals who are getting ready to manage large projects would also greatly benefit from the book.

> **Rajesh Hukku,** Chairman and Managing Director,
> i-flex Solutions Limited

A consultant builds multiple bridges: with himself, with his team and with his clients, to reach defined goals. **Beyond Code** is all about what it takes to build these bridges: listening to others, building a credible personal brand, building lasting relationships with clients and your team, building your learning curve, building leadership, sensibly bold strategy and unwavering commitment. This book is an investment in yourself.

> **S. Ramadorai,** CEO and MD, Tata Consultancy Services

Business Influencers & Leaders

Through personal lessons and industry examples, Rajesh does an excellent job of illuminating the critical personal and professional qualities that lead to success in our industry.

Darlene K. Mann, CEO, Siperian, Inc.

Beyond Code is packed with insights for IT professionals at all levels. If you are good and want to become great, this is one book that you should NOT miss reading.

Kurt Garbe, Executive Consultant, Former CEO, Movaris, Inc., Former EVP - USWeb

Beyond Code is an excellent resource for consultants in any space. As a previous leader of multiple software consultancies, I wish this book had been available for my consultants. This book provides great insight into what makes a consultant successful.

Matt Filios, CEO, Sourcebeat Publishing, former CEO, Tsunami Consulting and Virtuas Solutions

I have worked with Rajesh and I can say that he practices the ideas and behaviors that he shares in **Beyond Code**—it made him a stand-out in the IT consulting game. It was in the days before he founded CIGNEX, but it was evident then that his professional principles were guiding him to rise above the crowd, and lift his team and clients as well.

Sean Martin, VP Product Management, KnowNow Inc.

Entrepreneurs

It is the perfect book to take along on any business trip. And even if that trip isn't about business, **Beyond Code** will quickly turn it into one.

Chris Pirillo, Internet Entrepreneur

The book that you read more than once and keep for yourself is this one. It contains some of the key nuances that take most consultants, years, if not decades to understand.

Mitchell Levy, Partner, CEOnetworking

Different, captivating, a must read. A hand book or play book if you will for anyone wanting to be effective in today's fast paced global market place.

Paul D'Souza, Founder, The Wha-Dho Institute

Rajesh provides practical tools and unique insights for IT professionals to set higher standards and excel in the fast growing global IT services industry.

Vallal Jothilingam, CEO, The Game Called Life Company

Investors

A great book on the "soft" skills needed to be truly successful and satisfied in software consulting and in life. I recommend it to anyone with a career in software technology.

Shomit Ghose, Venture Coach, ONSET Ventures

I personally have watched Rajesh grow from an IT consultant to a powerful and visionary leader. He walks his talk and is committed to personal growth and learning!

Kannan Ayyar, Investor, Entrepreneur, Executive

BEYOND CODE

Learn to distinguish yourself in 9 simple steps!

Rajesh Setty

 SelectBooks, Inc.

BEYOND CODE: Learn to Distinguish Yourself in 9 Simple Steps
©2005 by Rajesh C.Setty

This edition published by SelectBooks, Inc.
For information address SelectBooks, Inc., New York, New York

First Edition

ISBN 1-59079-102-9

Library of Congress Cataloging-in-Publication Data

Setty, Rajesh, 1970-
  Beyond code : learn to distinguish yourself in 9 simple steps! / Rajesh C. Setty ; edited by Karthik Sundaram.-- 1st ed.
      p. cm.
  ISBN 1-59079-102-9 (hardbound : alk. paper)
 1. Leadership. 2. Management. 3. Success in business. I. Title.

HD57.7.S465 2005
650.1--dc22

2005018105

Printed in the United States of America
10 9 8 7 6 5 4 3 2 1

For my wife **Kavitha**,
and our son **Sumukh**.

Photo credit: Allison Shirreffs

FOREW O R D

IT professionals have discovered the most exciting industry in the world. And so it will remain for years to come. The problem: A lot of smart and hard working people, from every corner of the globe, have figured out the same thing at the same time. Moreover, industry volatility (think Oracle-Peoplesoft) is here to stay.

It has long been my contention that we are engulfed in a "white collar revolution." That between industry chaos, technology that takes over rote work and offshoring, simply being "smart," "showing up" and "doing good work" will not guarantee a job-- especially an exciting one. My code phrase for all this, coined about five years ago, is ... DISTINCT OR EXTINCT.

Speaking of code, my purpose here is to provide a ringing endorsement for Rajesh Setty's *Beyond Code*. It is a Gem!

Beyond Code makes my point, tailored brilliantly to IT professionals: Distinct or extinct! Even if you are a happy camper at a big and mostly invulnerable company, you simply must take immediate charge of your "practice." Another of my code phrases for this is ... become Brand You. That's a management-speak way of saying that you had better have a clear mark of distinction brilliantly communicated, both in terms of Content and your Professional Approach to developing and nurturing Client Relations. Sure, those "clients" today may simply be project peers at your company. But tomorrow you may well be fired, and today's "mere" peer may be a project manager at a new company on the lookout for Talent. In short, both the Theory and the Practice prescribed in this book are right on. Read it as if your life depends on it. It does!

TOM PETERS

CONTENTS

Prologue

Life is a series of projects

Whether we want to admit it or not, we are always in the middle of one or more projects in our life. Where we are headed in our life is largely dependent on how successful we are in these projects.

Life would be simple if all our projects were humming along well and we were exceeding expectations of key stakeholders. Unfortunately, this may not be the case in most of our lives. Most of our projects are running late, costing more, or both. There is a constant pressure internally and externally to give more, perform better, improve efficiency, and increase effectiveness. This very pressure has pushed many of us into a trap of working hard towards acquiring what I call "short term skills," i.e., becoming experts in certain skills that are currently "hot" in the market, only to realize later that the relevance of these skills quickly fades away. The sad part, though, is that we don't realize this when we are in the trap.

Imagine repeating this cycle a few times in our lives. Add family, raising kids, mini crises, endless meetings, business travel, vacations and so on to this mix. If something or someone does not awaken us, we will soon hit 40, and begin to wonder what exactly happened to our lives. We then look for someone or something to blame for where we are.

Having lived and worked in five different countries, I can tell you with confidence that this problem is global, and people fall into the same trap everywhere. Our efforts keep yielding short-term results, and it's so easy to miss the big picture. Think about this question: how many skills are you pursuing and/or sharpening that will take more than a few years to yield their results? Probably not many! We want results NOW!

We have become a world of "instant gratification junkies." They say that even if we were to win the rat race, it's of no use as it just proves that we are rats. How do we get out of this rat race and escape from being swept into the tsunami of commoditization?

We are smart people, and we know that if we continue to do the same things that we have done, we will continue to get the same results. We also know that we need to do different things and distinguish ourselves in order to get superior results in our life. It seems easy, but we know that it's not. We need tools and insights that will help us distinguish ourselves. We also need the discipline to practice them almost on a daily basis. In **Beyond Code**, I have put together a set of such insights and practices from my notes and cheat sheets collected over the last ten years.

Even during the swamping project periods, it is critical that we come up for air, look around, and wend our way back to our paths. This book will hopefully help us—the sinking tribe of project consultants—come up easily for that gulp of fresh air.

BEYOND CODE

Learn to distinguish yourself in 9 simple steps!

Get the most out of this book

You are often at a crossroad: there is the comfort of your status quo, and yet there is a yearning to achieve more. And you believe you can. I have been there and have moved on. And from this experience, I have learned.

Here is what you can expect to get out of this book:

Tools to get more out of your time

Insights to pack more value into every hour of your consulting engagement

Methods to Identify and leverage all your resources

Ways to increase your Likeability Index

Strategies to improve your listening

And many more. This book will take you between three to six hours to complete depending on how fast you read and how actively you participate in some of the exercises outlined. The price you paid for this book represents only a small part of your investment. Your time has value.

Return on Investment (ROI) is a key concept in business, and reading should be no different. I aim to ensure that you get the right ROI from this book. How? Let us go through an ROI exercise quickly. Fill up the appropriate values for each of the items below:

Your spending	Value
a. Cost of the book (amount paid by you)	$
b. Number of hours that you think are required to read the book first time	
c. Your hourly rate	$
d. Total time investment (b*c)	$
e. Miscellaneous (coffee or other expenses when you are reading this book)	$
Total Investment (a+d+e)	$

As the author, I have invested many hours and dollars in bringing this book to you. My ROI, as an author, occurs when you recommend this book to a friend or gift a copy of it. Nothing happens from a one-sided effort. I invite you to a partnership for the next few hours (whenever you are reading this book) and make it our common goal to succeed. I am sure you believe in teamwork and from now on, we both are a team to create a success story: YOURS! Let us agree to some ground rules on working towards getting the most out of this book:

Take this seriously: While my first few published works were fiction, I want to tell you that this book is not fiction. You will gain more out of this book, if *you* put more into it. You calculated your total investment in the exercise above, and that's the most you can lose. How much can you personally gain by applying these principles in your life? Well, you won't discover that answer, unless you try.

Clarify your objectives: You picked up this book to get something out of it for yourself; *not* to find out if *I* know anything about what I am saying in this book. We tend to judge the messenger, rather than focus on the message. It is your investment that is at stake and let us both work towards maximizing it.

Believe: You must believe that this book could help you reach the next level. In the end, if this turns out wrong, you know what you lost (your investment) but let's not worry about that now.

Participate!: Each chapter ends with an activity that shows you how to apply the principle in life. You might be tempted to read through the book without trying the exercises. However, you would miss much of the value the book can offer you. If you bought a Dummy's guide on swimming, you wouldn't dive into the Pacific Ocean for your first swim. You would practice your new skill in a safe place, like a pool. Your participation in the exercises is as critical.*

*All exercises in this book are available as easy downloads from www.lifebeyondcode.com

Personalize this read: Start making notes in the book (underline important points, mark comments on the side, highlight interesting sections, and so on.) as you progress. So, next time when you really want to revisit, it will be a breeze and will take a fraction of time that you took reading it the first time.

Have the right expectations: Books have changed people's lives in the past. Personally, I have been touched, moved and inspired by many good books. Expect that you will be touched and moved by some of the concepts outlined in this book. I am not saying that you have to agree with everything that I have written. If you agree with a concept, then start applying it in your life. You know your investment and the first step is to get the right returns for it. Let us start on this wonderful journey. Thank you for this opportunity to partner with you in creating a new reality for you.

Beyond Code: The Framework

If life is a game, this book will provide you tools to help you succeed and win. I believe that there are two kinds of games that we are involved in:

1. Inner Game: We all play this internal game with ourselves. I remember a quote from Covey "All things are created twice. Once in your mind. Once in the real world."

2. Outer Game: We play this game with the external world. No one is an island. Our relationship with the external world plays an important role in our overall success.

These are some basic rules about the games:

1. Both games are important.

2. Mastery in one game does not automatically qualify you to attain mastery in the other one.

3. One game is not easier than the other.

4. The quality of our game is directly proportional to the quality of our playbook.

The Inner Game

The Inner Game is where we have the most control. The

components of the Inner Game can be mastered alone. One of the key difference between winners and losers is the way winners look at some important things. Winning at the inner game requires you to look at life and work differently than others.

Learn: As a consultant, you spend much of your time creating and delivering projects. You probably also take time to learn new skills that will help you complete future projects. However, successful consultants also invest time to grow themselves in fundamental ways—such as learning how to build long-term relationships, being congruent, developing one's strengths, and keeping a scorecard.

Laugh: Even smart people can goof up occasionally. It's human to make mistakes, but you need to know how to handle these mistakes. If you handle your errors poorly, you can create a ruckus in your life. When you goof up (and it will happen), laugh at yourself and move on.

Look: You can easily differentiate yourself by looking beyond the expected. There are plenty of opportunities for people who know where to look.

Lasting Impression: Every engagement offers you the opportunity to make a lasting impression. So, make a decision to add significant value and noticeable impact through your effort. You will discover multiple rewards every time that you practice this discipline.

Love: Do you love your job? Many people answer that question with a "yes, but..." reply. No matter how you personally choose to answer this question, you will find that you have plenty of your reasons for your decision.

When you make a choice, your mind starts looking for evidence that supports your choice. Your mind focuses on reasons that support your choice and filters out other evidence. If you decide that you love your job, it will affect how you perceive your job. Your choice affects how you will view your colleagues and how you perceive everyday workplace situations.

The Outer Game

The Outer Game is a contact sport. Winning in this game involves people other than you. The key to winning the outer game is in mastering the relationship with the external world.

Leverage: When we work for a company, it is important to know that none of us are as smart individually as all of us combined. While this is true, this concept works only if everyone leverages the group's strengths. Most people understand the concept of leverage but very few people use it well. Ask yourself whether you fully draw upon all the resources that are available to you today?

Likeability: If we are likeable, people will often bend rules and make exceptions for us. Things seem easier for people who are likeable. If we are not likeable, we have a rough road ahead. Your likeability goes beyond just your character or your competence. You have to work to increase your likeability.

Listen: We all know the importance of listening well. Few of us can practice it consistently. Most of us have selective listening capabilities and we listen to only those things that will support our earlier conclusions. Start listening to start succeeding.

Lead: Leadership is not tied to a position. If you want to lead, look for gaps in your organization and start trying to fill them. Leadership can be as simple as filling in the blanks. Everyone's life is filled with leadership moments—moments where you can emerge as a leader. If you are ready, you can take advantage of the leadership moments in your life.

A mind map of getting the most out of Beyond Code

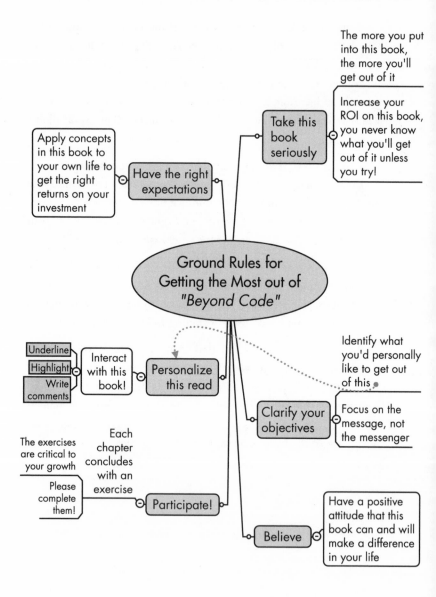

Distinguish Yourself

"Be Different!"

E asily said. What do I mean by it? Try "de-commoditization." As one among the millions who make up the services industry, how are you going to be seen valuable to your company or the company you seek to work at? Are you just another body that brings in either a particular knowledge base or skill set? Or are you something else?

There are books that have hyped up the character and competence issues in the job market. While I agree that it is a killer combination, banking solely on these is not going to get us where we want to be. This combination is now taken for granted-quite like an admission ticket to the park. We are not even allowed inside without these under our belt-and just these alone will only put us alongside a commodity crowd where we will be part of the statistics. We have to play by very different rules to "de-commoditize" ourselves to win.

Commodity stuff is boring

An automobile is a transport mechanism that takes you from point A to point B-commodity stuff, right? That said, why does a BMW sell you a car priced at $30,000-plus? At some point, Rolls Royce was known to have interviewed potential buyers before even agreeing to sell them a car! Auto manufacturers have made the automobile more than just a point-to-point transport mechanism. They add features to the car, engines and interiors to the point that now it is your personalized transport mode. You decide what options go into it. And pay for it. It is your personal statement. Take watches. Or clothes. Or even your home. To all material assets, consumer companies have transferred brand values that now you seek to own, so you can stand on these stilts and raise yourself above the crowd.

Apply the same principles to yourself. You are your greatest asset. Do you want to feel different by showing off the "objects" that you own or do you have plans to overhaul yourself so that you as a person are above the commodity crowd? What could you learn or do that will bring that special "you" to the table?

> To all material assets, consumer companies have transferred brand values that now you seek to own... but what is your personal brand?

Watch your decisions

No decision is small or insignificant. Your life and your destiny are shaped by decisions you make everyday. John Maxwell, noted leadership guru, said "Give me a day with you. I will be with you for one full day observing what you do without asking you any questions. You don't have to tell me anything. Just allow me to observe what you do, what decisions you take, and how you respond to situations. You continue to do what you would have done as if I was not there. At the end of the day, I will tell you where you are going." Something to think about!

Look back at your life and review some of the key decisions you made that got you where you are today. Now, think about some of the key decisions that you are going to make in the next few months.

Do you think that that these decisions will move you closer to where you want to be and what you want to become? Think through the possibilities that will open up if you made some changes to the qualities of your decisions. Take some risk, and try new things. If you do what you have always done, you know what you are getting, but you may never know what you missed until you truly try new things.

Know your destination

It has been found that only three percent of us on this planet have written goals. One simple way for you to be part of the elite group is to just sit down, take a piece of paper and start writing your goals. There is an old story: a disciple goes to his teacher and asks him what books he should be reading. The teacher asks back, "That depends on what you want to be when you grow up." The disciple thinks about it for a second and says, "You know, I really don't know." The teacher quickly remarks, "Then it really doesn't matter. Pick up any book and you should be fine."

If you don't know where you are going, you will find very little help and a lot of frustration. Imagine this—when you reach any destination, you may find that it is not the place where you wanted to be. Isn't it interesting to know that if you focus and work on it, it will take only a few hours to come up with a set of goals for yourself? You may also know that if you spend these two hours productively, you will be doing yourself a great favor. You can channel your energy the right way for the next few years. If this concept is so easy to understand why is that people don't take up the time to work on their goals?

Here are a few reasons. See if any of them are familiar.

You have other pressing needs. The moment you take care of them, you will work on your goals.

Reality: That day will never come. You will always have pressing needs. Wake up!

You want to be 100% sure that what you think your goal is what you want. This is your life and you want to be sure about your goals.

Reality: You can never be 100% sure of anything in the future. Make up your mind RIGHT NOW! You can always change it. It's your life!

You may be wrong.

Reality:Yes. And so what?

You want to keep your options open.

Reality: You can have goals without being attached to them. When something better comes up in your life along the way, you decide and take actions to do the right thing.

The idea is to stand up for something; otherwise you will fall for anything. Can you imagine boarding a train and trying to buy a ticket without knowing where to go? Before you read the next chapter, take a few minutes to identify what you want to become in the next few years.

> • • •
>
> If you don't know where you are going, you may find that where you reached is not the place where you wanted to be.

Stay the course

People just give up too soon. You can be different simply by staying the course for a longer time. Executing a plan is hard work. If you want to accomplish anything significant, you need to be ready for surprises (good and bad) along the way. Giving up is easy. Smart people always find a reasonable justification (a.k.a. smart excuses) for not staying the course. The next time you feel like giving up, decide to stay on for just a bit longer. It will make a huge difference!

Command a premium

Here are two questions that may seem unrelated but there is a reason for asking them. (Believe me, there is a connection between them.)

1. Have you ever felt that you are not receiving the right value for your work?

2. Have you seen people paying a premium price for branded products?

Most often, I get a "Yes" for both the questions. Now, here is the connection. You too can get a premium (higher value than what you are actually worth) if you truly build a powerful personal brand.

The power of consumer brands is creating shortcuts for people. They create defaults (obvious choices) for people who don't have the time to think through all options, or analyze the true value of what the brand is offering. It is no different for personal brands. The reliability and dependability are taken for granted when you have a personal brand. This provides you with a powerful time advantage.

You now don't have to spend time trying to prove that you are capable. That is taken for granted. This saved time can be invested in creating an even superior personal brand.

Answer this question: Who are you?

It seems like an easy question to answer, but there is a twist to it. Answer the question without borrowing your company's brand. In other words, describe who you are without mentioning your company. This becomes quite hard for many people, as they have never thought about the value or the need for building a personal brand.

> Your reliability, integrity, and dependability are taken for granted when you have a personal brand: a powerful time advantage.

To draw some inspiration, take a look at some prominent people: Tom Peters, Gary Hamel, Seth Godin, Suze Orman and others. They have built phenomenal personal brands for themselves. Many of them have their own companies or consult for other companies. In all their cases, it is their company or client who draw upon their personal brands, and not vice versa. Their personal brands are much larger than the companies they are associated with. You don't have to build a globally recognizable personal brand for yourself. These people set the benchmarks—something that you can draw inspiration from, and execute within your possibilities.

When I talk about personal brands, the most common reaction is, "They can do it. They are in a different business. There is no way I can do it by myself!" I beg to differ. A wise man once said, "It doesn't matter what you do. If you are the very best at whatever you do, you WILL make a name for yourself." Three examples worth mentioning:

Building a chair: What can be more common than building

a chair? Seth Godin talks about a person who specializes in building chairs by hand: one chair at a time. Each chair is unique, and I believe he will create only one chair of its kind at a time. If you want a chair built for yourself, you need to wait about nine months to get yours. You should also be ready to fork over $90,000 for a chair.

Builder Extraordinaire: If you are a builder, how can you create a brand for yourself? Impossible? Think again. Take a look at what my friend Tim Carter, builder extraordinaire, has created for himself. His website, Ask the Builder, (www.askthebuilder.com) is one of the most visited construction sites on this planet. His columns are featured in 42 newspapers, and several radio stations air his programs on building issues. Tim is an epitome of what a builder could do.

Startup expert: I have a friend in India who is currently heading an offshore subsidiary of a U.S.-based consulting firm. He says, "I am an expert in getting startups off the ground. I provide that expertise to a company in the U.S."

What can **you** do today to build or enhance your personal brand? Remember that nobody will be more interested than yourself on building your personal brand. It is your sole responsibility to take this up on a priority basis. Take personal accountability for building your brand. The only problem with investing in your personal brand building is that it takes a long time to get some payback.

Break some rules, create some wealth

Conformity provides an illusion of guarantee. Here is a simple rule that conformity teaches. Identify someone who has done exactly what you want to do; who has achieved what you want to achieve. Ask him or her what exactly he or she did and try to follow those same steps. Success should follow, right? Wrong! Nothing could be farther than this from truth. Here are some reasons why you may achieve different results from what the other person did:

You are not the same person: You both will respond and react to outcomes very differently.

Contexts change: The contexts you both are operating in will be different. The people around you, the culture you live in, and the major events of the day will shape you. Some events, like 9/11, reshape the world in an instant. Other issues, like outsourcing grow over time.

No guarantees: There were no guarantees for your role model, and so are there no guarantees for you.

Guy Kawasaki, compulsive entrepreneur, tells a story about ice:
In the late 1800s, there was a thriving ice industry in the northeast. Companies would cut blocks of ice from frozen lakes and ponds, and sell them around the world. The largest known single shipment was 200 tons shipped to India. Only a hundred tons got to India—the rested melted off enroute—but this was enough to make a profit. These ice harvesters, however, were put out of business by companies that invented mechanical icemakers. It was no longer necessary to cut and ship ice because companies could make it in any city during any season. Then the refrigerator companies put the icemakers out of business. If it was convenient to make ice at a manufacturing plant, imagine how much better it was to make ice and create cold storage in everyone's home. You would think that the ice harvesters would see the advantages of making ice locally, and adopt this technology. However, all they could think about was around what was already known: better saws, better storage, and better transportation. Then you would think that the icemakers would see the advantages of refrigerators and adopt this technology. The truth is that the ice harvesters couldn't embrace the unknown, and jump from their curve to the next.

People think twice about taking the road less traveled. There are no guarantees on the beaten path, and you are part of the statistics on that road. Start taking calculated risks. Change the rules or create new ones. You will be glad you did! Playing safe is the most risky option you have.

Be an innovator

If you are not an inventor, the next best thing would be to be an innovator. Innovators make a huge impact on the society in very little time. Innovation is the quickest way to "de-commoditize" yourself and your company. You can find numerous books on the topic, and you could start by reading them.

The other simpler approach is to start observing all the startups that are being founded in Silicon Valley and elsewhere. Startups are a phenomenal demonstration of innovation. While there are hundreds or thousands of run-of-the-mill startups that are trying to take advantage of an opportunity, there are a handful that start with the premise that they will change the rules or create new rules.

Observe the value propositions of these companies keenly. Be a student of these propositions. These founders saw something that the others didn't.

If you do this consistently, your thinking sharpens and you will start looking at things in a different fashion.

The Innovation bug will bite you.

THE INNER GAME

- Learn • Laugh • Look
- Leave a lasting impression • Love

On Learning

"The illiterate of the 21st century will not be those who cannot read and write, but those who cannot learn, unlearn, and relearn."

Alvin Toffler

"An organization's ability to learn, and translate that learning into action rapidly, is the ultimate competitive advantage."

Jack Welch

"Experience is a hard teacher because she gives the test first, the lesson afterwards."

Vernon Saunders Law

"The man who does not read good books has no advantage over the man who cannot read them."

Mark Twain

"It is the mark of an educated mind to be able to entertain a thought without accepting it."

Aristotle

Learn

As consultants, we want our current projects to go well and exceed expectations. However, we also need to prepare ourselves for future projects. Future projects may require us to know skills that are very different from the ones we use in our current projects. How can we find time to prepare ourselves for the future and still meet our project deadlines? The only way to ensure that our skills remain relevant is through continuous, never-ending learning.

When we choose	The result is
Extreme focus on short-term delivery	Short-term success Future success not guaranteed Decreased resilience
Extreme focus on preparing for the future	Short-term failure Uncertainty: Are we playing your cards right?

Acknowledging the need for continuous learning, the next obvious question is, what should we learn next? Let's look at some skills that can help you make both your current and future projects successful:

The art of building long-term relationships
It's been said that there are only two kinds of relationships: long-term and very long-term. A simple way to create relationships that last is to constantly add value to the other party.

We constantly face the temptation to ask, "What's in it for me?" But if you can resist that thought, you will find powerful forces of reciprocation entering your life. There's an old saying: "When you think you need a friend, it's too late." But if we create new friends continually, we wouldn't have to worry about that question. If you remember, the rule of "six degrees of separation" says that any two people in the world are separated by (or connected by) six links at the most. This means that just six people between you can connect you and somebody else whom you have never met. While it seems like an attractive concept, remember that the strongest links we form are the ones closest to us. Relationships provide a significant competitive advantage.

A word of caution: Every relationship that we want to nurture will take away a piece from us—our time, our heart, and our mind. Hence, it is very important to choose who we want to build a relationship with.

Identify your strengths and go with them

When we are operating on our strengths, we are at our very best. When we're operating from our weaknesses, we'll tend to feel—and will be perceived as—less confident. And we might not enjoy those activities. The key to cultivating confidence is by spotting our strengths and managing our weaknesses. One way to become more aware of our strengths is to notice and carefully reflect on the times when we feel most "in a flow." Whenever we are assigned a job, we should look at all of the components, and ask ourselves what portions we can accomplish with our strengths. Consider those parts of the task "covered." We'll need to manage the remaining tasks. Being unaware of this need is a serious weakness. After we've identified our strengths and weaknesses, we should learn to play with our strengths. You should spend the most significant portion of your day on activities that access your strengths. And your growth plan should aim at further enhancing those strengths.

Learn to communicate well

If we don't have something and must get it from others, we'll need to ask for it. Whether we get it or not will depend (apart from other factors) on the quality of communication we are going to have with the other person. The purpose of communication is to arrive at a common understanding on a particular topic. Communication has two components—sending and receiving.

> You have no control over how your messages are received, so you must fill them with maximum clarity.

The tendency is to take responsibility for one part of the process, but not the other.

For example, when we compose an email to a client or colleague, we should try pausing for a moment before we hit "send." Reread the message from the recipient's viewpoint. What will he or she understand and feel while reading our email is important. If it doesn't communicate our message clearly, we should then take the time to re-write it; and repeat the exercise

©2004 Don Moyer (don@amsite.com)

until we get it right. We really have no control over how our messages are received. So we must take every possible step to fill them with clarity, based on our knowledge of the recipients.

Whether you are writing, meeting face to face, talking on the phone, or delivering a training program, remember that the more you know about your audience, the more power you will have. Take the time to know and care about the people that you communicate with regularly: it will mean a lot to them, and it will make your life easier.

Learn to be congruent

When our words and actions don't match, we not only surprise people, we will also confuse them. Incongruent behavior is a result of trivializing things in life. We may think that it's all right to treat somethings trivially. What seems trivial to one person may be very important to the other person. Moreover, when our words and thoughts affect others, nothing is trivial. No promise is small. Earlier in my consulting career, I was a project manager for a large multinational bank in Singapore. A report was due one Friday, and not surprisingly, I slipped on the due date. The following Monday, the manager talked to me. He came straight to the point. "I am responsible for six projects, and yours is one of them. I have received status reports from four project managers, but two of you did not send me yours. Now I have to send a consolidated report and an updated dashboard to my boss every Monday morning. I am not just delayed here; I also have to meet with you both to explain the problem and justify why you need to keep your promises. I hope you understand what's happening here." That was the last time I delayed any status reports to anyone. The consequence of incongruence is that it makes us very unpredictable and untrustworthy.

Setting the right expectations

Most projects fail because people don't share the same expectations. By setting the right expectations, we are setting ourselves up to exceed them. If you are going to execute on a project that someone else sold, you are already at a disadvantage. Someone else has set the expectations for the client, and you have to exceed them. It requires great skill and trustworthiness to reset the expectations closer to reality. Let us consider a simple case and look at what happens on a daily basis. A client asks us for the delivery date of some document's. We think that this project should take two days (16 hours), and we promise to deliver the document in three days. Come three days, the document is not ready, and we are wondering what went wrong. Here is one analysis that might explain what could have gone wrong in this situation:

> *a. We really didn't have eight hours in a day to work on this document. In fact, we don't have eight full hours to work on any one project. Let us conservatively say that we had only six hours to work on this project. We lose two hours per day on general activities.*
>
> *b. A lot of other activities happened during those three days. Mini-crises and urgent matters consume another hour a day.*
>
> *c. We had made other promises to other people. We need to fulfill them, and that takes another hour per day.*

So, in a three-day engagement, we might truly have had only twelve hours to work on a document that needed at least sixteen hours to complete. Is it any wonder that we were delayed in completing the document? The solution would have been to think through this scenario before signing up for a delivery date. This may seem easy, but it requires you to make a serious shift in your mindset.

When people come to us with a request, they will fetch an immediate answer (a delivery date). We need to learn how to reset people's expectations. If we are very clear on all the outcomes expected of us, and how our time is going to be spent in the next couple of days, it is easy to explain and re-prioritize our delivery schedules. This requires us to be proactive and beware of all our commitments.

Keep a scorecard

All of us can plan and create wish lists. I am not undermining the need to have goals and plans. They are a prerequisite to get somewhere. However, execution is as important as planning.

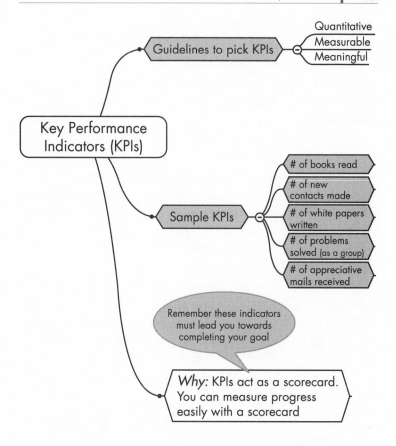

Keeping a scorecard to check and know your progress is vital.

At the risk of over simplifying, I want to present a Seven Step plan to help us do this.

1. Know where we are
2. Know what we want to become
3. Identify the gap (what is missing in the equation)
4. Define an action plan to get where we want to go
5. Identify key performance indicators
6. Keep a scorecard to measure progress and feedback
7. Modify the action plan based on the feedback

It is important to ensure that your scorecard has "measurable" indicators. This means that all five indicators should be some measurable numbers. Examples of Key Performance Indicators (KPIs) are as follows:

Number of books read

Number of new contacts made

Number of white papers written

Number of problems solved (in a discussion group)

Number of appreciative mails received

Find performance indicators that will lead you toward your goal. Resist the temptation to create more than five KPIs. If you have more than five, then pick your top five. Decide how and when you want to track these indicators. In many cases, you may decide a month is a reasonable frequency. If you want to be super-effective, ask a close friend to hold you accountable for these numbers and your whole learning process.

Look at the big picture

Anyone who can solve a business problem or unlock a business opportunity wins big bucks. Your work will be a piece in the bigger puzzle. Develop the curiosity to know what the entire puzzle looks like and how your piece will fit in it. The ability to understand and contribute to the big picture may be the single biggest differentiator that you can develop. Here are some questions you can ask to get the big picture:

1. What is the business need? Why are we embarking on this project?
2. What are the success criteria for this project? How will we recognize success?
3. What is this project's expected outcome?
4. How will this project impact the rest of the business?
5. What do others expect out of me?
6. How many people or groups are involved in the full project? Where does my group fit in this project? What will others expect from us?
7. Why is this project important to the organization?
    a. To save money?
    b. To increase revenues?
    c. To gain a competitive advantage?
8. Who will be affected by this project?
9. Who are the key stakeholders for this project?

10. How will other people recognize my success or failure? How will people measure my contribution?

When you know the big picture, you have an unfair advantage. You will have more opportunities to go above and beyond the call of duty. It also provides clear meaning to your daily activities. Take time to learn your clients. What are their value propositions? What industries do they operate in? What are their business models? How do they make money? Who are their competitors?

If your client is a publicly traded company, then you can get a lot of information about them on the Web. If the client is a privately-held company, then explore website, search on the Web, read their press releases, and even talk to some of the company's long-term employees.

Read the right material

There is an information overload today, and it is only going to worsen. I have a simple rule of reading one book a week—about 50 books a year. Some weeks I succeed, and some weeks I fail in reading a book. But in the overall sum up, I make it to 50 in a year. I build my reading list based on recommendations I get from those whom I respect. Coaches, mentors, other successful people, and other books help me develop my list. Every time I meet someone I respect, I ask them what they are reading and why they chose to read those books. Most people happily share their reading list. Three ways to be updated in less time:

Read book summaries: rather than the complete books. This is a great "try before you buy" model. If you like the summary, you can invest in the full book.

Audio books: If your job involves travel, audio books can help you get the most out of your time on the road. Most audio books are now available in MP3 format and can be easily downloaded into an MP3 player.

Join Book Clubs: Join book clubs in your area that cover the kind of books that you want to read. If there are none, team up with a few of your like-minded friends and start a book club.

Create the urgency to learn

Our clients often expect us to deliver flawless results. Everyone around will create an urgency for us to deliver. Very rarely does anyone force us to prepare and learn for the future. People seem to operate by Newton's Third Law: "Action and reaction are equal and opposite." People want to see immediate results for every action they take. Nature, though, operates in an evolutionary fashion. It takes nine months for a baby to gestate, and it takes years for a tree to be formed.

When you start investing in yourself, you develop your character and become a better person. However, it takes a long time to see results. Newton's Law still is applicable—but with a time lag. In fact, it gets better: if you consistently apply the right actions over a long period of time, we start seeing disproportionate results. However, it requires internal motivation, enormous self-discipline and resolve to create the urgency to learn today. We need to create the urgency to learn what is required for tomorrow. Be proactive.

Use the right tools

If all this seems like a lot of work, know that there is help out there, in the form of tools and techniques. Here are a few tools that will accelerate your journey to the next level:

Music for Learning: I have been fascinated by accelerated learning techniques. Music increases the effectiveness of your learning and saves you time. Several schools use Baroque music in the background when teachers deliver their lectures and seminars. It works! My friend Steven Halpern is a world-renowned authority on music for accelerated learning. A CD costs less than $20, but the value it brings is priceless.

Mindmapping: Whether we are brainstorming an idea, writing a report, or creating an outline for a book, "mindmapping" will help. It is one of the simplest, yet most powerful, tools a person can have in his or her creative toolbox. Mindmapping is a non-linear way of organizing information and a technique that allows you to capture the natural flow of your ideas. We have included mindmaps throught out this book, and more are available for download from www.lifebeyondcode.com for your reference.

Adapt

Charles Darwin proposed the theory of "survival of the fittest." For most of us, this needs to be modified to "survival of the most adaptable." In the last ten years, I have seen only a small percentage of consultants who settled into long-term projects. Most consultants hop from project to project, with one or more of the following changes:

Team

Client

Nature of the problem being solved

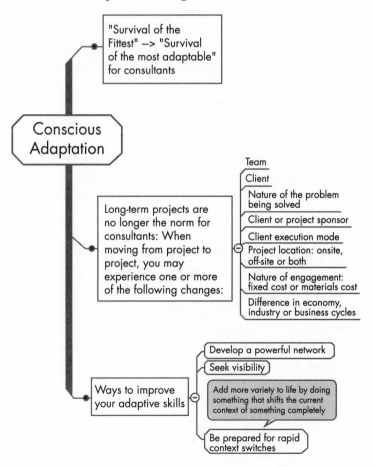

Client project sponsor
Project execution mode: on site, off site, or a
combination of both
Project location
Nature of engagement

Additionally, overarching parameters such as economy, industry cycles, and business context changes will affect almost every project over time. Talk about change! This is almost like drinking from a fire hose. The ability to adapt and excel in the face of change is not a luxury—it is a fundamental requirement.

When we begin a new project on a Monday morning, the client expects us to be fully present and ready for the project. There is no concession or sympathy shown, even though we may have been in a different world the previous Friday. When we don't plan to adapt consciously, we are made to adapt to the situation by brute force. This means frustration, long hours, and sleepless nights.

Here are three steps that you can take to be ready:

1. *Seek information*: The first step in gaining control is to seek more information on the kind of projects for the next few months (if possible). With some research, this will provide you with early warnings of what is in store. We should not only seek knowledge from the projects but also from the trends that are looming.

2. *Develop a powerful network*: The second step is to develop a powerful network. (More about this in the chapter titled "Leverage.") You never know when you will need it.

3. *Be prepared for rapid context switches*: Learn to be at ease with context switches. You can start small by introducing some variety into your life-pick up a habit, read some nonfiction, play a game, call a long-lost friend, or watch a horror movie. Do something that shifts the context completely. Once context switches become a part of our life, you will adapt to new situations more easily.

I LEARNED

Today's date: / /

My first job was that of a teacher. I observed that whenever I taught something to someone, the subject was clearer to me. This observation was validated by many others and I found that teaching is a great way of learning. Our action plan is to implement just that. Your task is to find someone to teach what you learned in this section.

Planning:

By when will you teach (date): / /

Who will you teach this to (name): _____

ACCOUNTABILITY REPORT

Find a friend who will help you to hold yourself accountable for this resolution. This is an important step. Please don't try to do it yourself. The process works great only if you enroll someone else to help you to be accountable. Now try to exceed the expectations. Share this with more than one person in your life. Your friend has to acknowledge that you have really done this.

S.No.	Date	Who did you teach?	What was the outcome?
1			
2			

Acknowledged By:

On Laughing

"Don't take life too seriously. You'll never escape it alive anyway."
Elbert Hubbard

"Throughout life people will make you mad, disrespect you and treat you bad. Let God deal with the things they do, cause hate in your heart will consume you too."
Will Smith

"Each morning when I open my eyes I say to myself: I, not events, have the power to make me happy or unhappy today. I can choose which it shall be. Yesterday is dead, tomorrow hasn't arrived yet. I have just one day, today, and I'm going to be happy in it."
"Groucho" Marx

"If you are going through hell, keep going."
Sir Winston Churchill

"Seventy percent of success in life is showing up."
Woody Allen

Laugh

I am fortunate to have lived and worked in five different countries during my consulting career. Some of my friends have lived in a lot more countries than I have. One common thread among all these people is that after a few years of living in different places, they become extremely adaptable.

My first job out of college was with a financial software company. I worked there for only about eighteen months as a programmer in their wholesale banking division, when I flew to Malaysia—my first trip abroad. It was all very exciting, to say the least. I was picked up from the airport and shown into a guesthouse that would later become my residence for the next two years. My office was supposed to be very close and I was given directions to walk to the office next morning. I wanted to make sure where I was and noted down the street address. "Jalan Sehala."

I reported at the office next day and spent the morning meeting people. At lunch, one of the friendlier acquaintances asked me where I was staying. I told him that I was staying at the company guesthouse. Apparently there were seven company guesthouses and wanting to be more specific, I said, "I am staying at the guest house on Jalan Sehala." People around the table started laughing, and I was a bit embarrassed. But I mustered the courage and plodded on, "Are there more than one guest houses in Jalan Sehala?" People continued to laugh even louder, and one of them finally stopped and explained that Jalan Sehala means a one-way street and in that area, every other street was a Jalan Sehala. I finally did manage to find my way back to the guesthouse later, and have traveled the beautiful Malaysian cities quite extensively in the years I spent there. A few years later I was in Paris to manage a six hundred-person sales force automation project for one of the largest companies in France. The day I landed, I was told that they had planned a "Requirements Definition Workshop" the next day to kick-start the project, and I was to prepare for that event. During dinner that night I figured out the lay of the land and found out the format of the workshops and the roles and responsibilities of people who were going to participate in the workshop. Before retiring for the night, I reviewed my material once again, and I was quite comfortable with the whole exercise.

The next morning, though, there was a new hurdle to cross. Of the 23 on the team, 22 couldn't (or wouldn't) speak English. And there I was, with a slick presentation—all in the Queen's *lingua franca*. Luckily, one spoke the language and was promptly honored to play interpreter. There were many "out-of-box" features in the enterprise application that we were planning to implement, and this involved a lot of explanation. The interpreter and I worked out a quick protocol. I would talk for a couple of minutes, and then the interpreter would translate.

And so we started. I spoke for two minutes and he spoke for two minutes. We alternated well and got into a rhythm. When there were questions, he would translate the question to me in English, and my response would be translated back to the group in French. However, the problem surfaced when I spoke for two minutes and he would speak for six or eight minutes. "Wow!" I thought, "What is he explaining so expansively? I had just explained a simple functionality." I had no way of finding out, while the session was in progress. Long story short-the next few hours went by with me sincerely hoping that the interpreter was doing his job right.

I smile when I think of those two incidents. I am sure you

have your own similar stories from your projects. Every such experience teaches us a valuable lesson that will help us be better prepared for future such surprises. It is important to observe and remember what goes on in your mind whenever you are in the middle of such an experience. Time and again, I have observed that people who are able to laugh at themselves make a lot more friends than others. They get along with clients more easily. There seems to be a strong link between this trait and a person's self esteem. People with a good dose of self-esteem can can laugh at themselves quite easily, and alternately, those who are comforable laughing at themselves tend to develop a healthy self-esteem. Now that we have established the need to be able to laugh at ourselves, what can we do to get started? Here are some thoughts and comments.

Focus on the character

There is so much focus on skills today that people are forgetting the foundation on which skills are built—character. The old saying has stood the test of time, "what you are speaks so loudly that I can't hear what you are saying." The temptation to focus on skills is high—with so much marketing and hype on developing them. And unfortunately, skills tend to show up results much faster than what strong character can.

Developing a strong character is hard work. There is no 99% great character. It is digital. Either you have it or you don't. You can't say, "I can compromise only for a while, and nobody will notice it." Our character is best defined by what you do when nobody is looking. A strong character will make you very comfortable with the most important person in our life—yourself! When you are very comfortable with yourself, you don't have a problem about laughing at yourself; and when you are able to laugh at yourself, other people are more comfortable with you.

Let go (sometimes!)

It's acceptable to let your guard down at times. Our clients are ultimately people and they want to see the human side of us. When we are sent on a project as an expert, the temptation is to don a "Superman" garb and to be at our best at all times. We all know how artificial this can be; there is no way anyone can know everything about everything. Relax and drop that Superman cape. When we are relaxed and approachable, people around us will respond accordingly.

Choose your company

Watch who you spend most of your time with; if your close friends take themselves very seriously, it may be hard to build any long-term relationships with them. Imagine a team where everyone takes his or her job seriously, but nobody takes himself seriously. Team members will be more open to give and receive feedback and the team performance inches up. When hiring new team members, we should check how comfortable they are about talking about their failures. Research says that we tend to hire fast and fire slow—we are better off hiring people with the right attitude; aptitudes will come.

Create a fun environment

A couple of posters that you will see in our office in Silicon Valley go like this:

> **Everyone here seems normal,**
> **until you get to know them.**
>
> **It is illegal to be normal and work here.**

There is one in the kitchen that says:

> **This is a self-cleaning kitchen.**
> **You eat. You clean.**

When we launched Cignex with only a handful of people, we decided lunch would be a special occasion for all of us to meet. It was potluck where everyone would partake from all the lunch boxes. Four years later the tradition still continues, and it has now become the part of our culture. The deal is simple. Whoever is in the office will participate in the potluck everyday. Lunch table discussions are rarely boring and people actually look forward to this session.

Discussions at this hour are always fun and rarely related to the business. People share their hobbies and talk about movies and sports; weekend plans are discussed. The conversations are unrestricted, and the whole session takes anywhere between 30 and 45 minutes. Time flies during this session, and people are amazingly refreshed when they return to work. The last time we conducted our employee meeting, we asked for three things that people liked about working with Cignex, and not surprisingly, the "group lunch" ranked on top.

You can initiate grassroot level efforts to bring about a change in you company, even if you are not part of the management. History is filled with numerous examples where simple grassroots initiatives in time became large corporate initiatives. Believe me, if you truly believe in your idea, if the initiative has the right intentions, and if you are willing to take full responsibility for the results, the only element pending is your full commitment to achieve the desired result.

Nobody cares

About you that is! Each person is more worried about himself or herself than about anybody else in this world. Nobody "really" cares about how you dress or what happened to you over the weekend, your toothache or your new car. Often, people are worried about what other people will think of them, and become increasingly conscious of every move. With the number of issues that people are dealing with in their lives, where do you think they have the time to think about you?

Whenever you hesitate extending your hand in a gathering for fear of being rejected, know that the other person is exactly in the same state. In effect, you are creating a deadlock between the two of you-each one is worrying about rejection from the other. It is a classic lose-lose situation. Being aware of just this one point will give you an amazing amount of power and a shot in the arm when it comes to networking. Your self-esteem will shoot up ten times. Common sense says that every person is unique and so are you. You are different from anyone else in this world and that in itself should provide you with a unique advantage that nobody else has. The "big win" comes when you know that it's OK to be YOU and you don't have to be some else to be accepted.

> You are different from anybody else in the world. That in itself is a unique advantage for you.

Rx for stress and failure

We don't have to look for stress or failure. Both of these will find us wherever we are. It is part of life. A healthy dose of stress, in fact, may be very good for health and growth. "Failure is the stepping stone of success," they say. Everyone knows that, but very few can deal with failure when it really strikes. Why is it so? Ask anyone who is extremely successful if they have ever failed in their life, and you will realize that their life was indeed spotted with successes and failures.

Can we look back at our lives and see the number of failures that we have gone through so far? Think about moments of time when those failures actually occurred. Some of them would have made us feel that it was the end of our career or even of our life. If we look back at the same failures today, we will not only laugh at them but will realize how silly we were to give them so much importance at that time. The next time you are faced with a failure, laugh and fast forward your life a few months ahead, when you will look back at this failure. Do you think you will feel the same as now about this failure? Probably not!

A seminar leader demonstrated this point beautifully. He asked the participants about watching their kids grow. "Did you guys remember those days when your kids were just learning to walk?" Most of the parents remembered about those experiences and nodded. The seminar leader continued, "Sometimes these kids fall down more than a hundred times before they could walk right. Do you agree?" Most of the parents nodded in agreement. "So," he said "when your kids fell down for the fiftieth time, why didn't you just feel that it's not worth taking the risk anymore and fifty was really too many times to learn just walking, and ask your kid to give up?"

There was a deep silence in the room. While I could see that nobody bought into the seminar leader's logic, I could also see many angry faces in the room, asking the leader silently, "Have you gone mad? How can you even think about asking such a question? I will not let go until my child learns how to walk—even if it takes a thousand attempts."

The seminar leader delivered the punch line, "Interestingly, I have not gotten one positive response to this question so far in my life. However, when it comes to your own life and your own goals, you start giving up after a few attempts. There is a far less commitment to your goals now, compared to the commitment about getting your baby to walk." It is really true that many of us give up the first time we fall down. In life, it is impossible NOT to fall down. In fact, it is not the falling down that is the problem. It is the self-talk when you fall down that is more important. Are you saying to yourself that you are a failure, or do you laugh, and decide to get up and start again every time you fall down?

Winners handle failure and stress very differently. How about you?

I LAUGHED

Today's date: / /

Remember two things—one from your childhood and one from your adult life where you goofed up. Laugh at yourself about what happened and share these incidents with a friend in the next 7 days.

Planning:

By when will you share these incidents (date): / /

Who will you share this with (name):

_____

ACCOUNTABILITY REPORT

Find a friend who will help you to hold yourself accountable for this resolution. This is an important step. Please don't try to do it yourself. The process works great only if you enroll someone else to help you to be accountable. Now try to exceed the expectations. Share this with more than one person in your life. Your friend has to acknowledge that you have really done this.

S.No.	Date	What did you share?	What was the outcome?
1			
2			

Acknowledged By:

On Looking

"When you innovate, you've got to be prepared for everyone telling you you're nuts."

Larry Ellison

"Intellectuals solve problems. Geniuses prevent them."

Albert Einstein

"Do not go where the path may lead, go instead where there is no path and leave a trail."

Casanova

"The most important thing in communication is to hear what isn't being said."

Peter Drucker

Look

L ook beyond what is expected out of you. You don't elicit a "wow!" by just delivering the expected outputs—you have to do something remarkable to receive the attention you so desire.

The quickest way to "de-commoditize" oneself is by finding out ways to deliver beyond what is expected of us. The first question that comes up is, "What do I look for?" followed by, "Where do I look for it?" Here are some thoughts:

Actively look for associations

Noted business guru Gary Hamel talks about "knowledge arbitrage" as one method of innovation. Knowledge arbitrage is basically borrowing a successful business concept from another industry and applying it in some fashion to your own industry, business or geography. You require a very inquisitive mind to take advantage of "knowledge arbitrage."

You have to relentlessly look for new associations, day in and day out. When executed properly, the results you achieve will be so phenomenal that others will soon think it was the only obvious way of doing something. Ask yourself, "Right. Anyone could have done it, but am I the first one to see it?" You can innovate when you look at something very differently than anyone else. Learn how to develop and leverage this skill. In my opinion, if you want to innovate, start actively looking for associations that have never existed before. How do you do this? There is no policy manual for this process, unfortunately—it comes with practice and you will get better at it as you start using your association skills.

Keep a relationship journal

We leverage the most from the relationships that we form in our life. Therefore, it is in our best interest that we do things that will enhance our ability to maintain solid relationships.

A relationship journal is a book (or a customized software application, if you are in that mode!) with one page dedicated to each of our close contacts or relationships. On the person's page, record everything that you know about this person and what you think is relevant. Record all information this person values most, and also what you think would help you associate this person with some other person or opportunity.

Some of the data points worth considering are:

place of birth
religion
places lived and worked
colleges attended
past work experience
hobbies and interests
close friends
likes and dislikes (eating, reading etc.)
values and beliefs
their work - what do they do for a living

Make no mistake. The relationship journal takes years to build and it is never "complete." As long as we keep "looking," we will keep "finding" interesting points about our close relationships that are worth "recording." Now, we must make it a point to regularly review this journal and add/modify information as and when we find it appropriate.

When you meet new people and you want to build a significant relationship with them, the first thing that should come to your mind is all the possible connections that you can make for them with other members in your relationship journal. This can only be meaningful if your relationship journal is current and accurate.

Look for connections that will yield maximum benefits to both parties. There should be a healthy value exchange for any relationship to sustain. Let the miracles begin! Don't let the simplicity of the process deter you from starting this wonderful journey. This process has far too many positive side effects to list here. Try this without asking what there is in it for you. You will get something only if you give. And this is giving at your best!

Look at your circle of possible influence

I have generously employed "knowledge arbitrage" from Stephen Covey's *Seven Habits of Highly Effective People* to demonstrate this concept. Look at your circle of influence with reference to your current project:

Now, let us look beyond this circle. Our circle of possible influence may be way beyond where our circle of influence lies. Remember that the commodity crowd struggles to make a difference in their "circle of influence." We have all the power if we excel in our circle of influence and start treading into the circle of "possible influence." There is a scarcity of people who operate in the circle of possible influence and as you all know very well, "scarcity shoots up value."

Your deliverables
Your team mates
Your project sponsor
Tools & technologies you use
Departments you affect
Geographies you are involved in

Circle of influence

Your Circle of Influence

Members from other project teams
Projects & other technologies
Ongoing Projects
Resources used
Other departments, other geographies and players
Future project roadmaps & integration

Circle of possible influence

Look for simplicity

There are several books written on simplicity. I want to cover the basics here. The most precious commodity in every person's life is "Time." We become very valuable if we can find ways to help people leverage their time better. I chose two things that can precisely do that-simplicity and clarity. If you can look for ways of enhancing both of them, you will be a hero wherever you are.

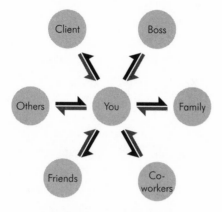

Reducing Clutter: The clutter in everyone's life is unbelievable. If one of your goals is to simplify "doing" business with you, you will save a lot of time for all parties involved. "You" here is both you as an organization, department or a business unit, and in another context, yourself as a person. The latter is more powerful. Examine all the interface points that exist between you and all other parties that you deal with. This is a sort of personal process reengineering exercise. There is a reason why all these interfaces exist. By looking for ways to simplify these interfaces, you and the party on the other end of the interface will benefit hugely. Here is a three step process for simplification:

Know why the interface exists: Who are the people involved, and what do they expect out of this interface? Know the expectations.

Establish rules of Engagement: What is the framework for interactivity and how do you handle exceptions?

Know where you are right now: Do either of you have the right tools to know where you are on all the engagements between the two of you? This is a kind of scorecard.

Look for clarity

Simplicity and clarity are related but they are not the same. Let's say you simplify a status reporting process by an email every week. You can send an unclear email on a Friday leading to a series of phone calls or an in-person meeting on Monday, defeating the whole purpose.

Get clarity in your work: Most people are not clear about what to do either on a Monday morning or throughout the week. Days, weeks, and months pass by in a busy blur, when you look back, you suddenly realize that you did not achieve anything significant. I am sure you don't want to remain in that camp. Clarity about your work will make your work more meaningful.

Enhance clarity in your communication: Stop for a minute before you send out that email. Reread what you have prepared. Think whether your communication will be interpreted the way you intended. If not, recreate your communication with better clarity. Communication that can be misinterpreted is worse than no communication.

Look for disproportionate returns

The hourly rate fee structure is the biggest joke in the consulting industry. Instead of working at increasing the hours we bill, we should look for ways of increasing the value we pack in an hour—the hourly rate will automatically go up. I have participated in hundreds of discussions that involve negotiating an hourly rate, and some patterns have not changed: once a client is convinced about the value you deliver, very rarely are they interested in lowering the hourly rate. Big bucks are in store for people who look for disproportionate returns for the invested resources (time, money, hardware, and software) for them as well as their clients. As long as the value rate is high, there will never be a problem with the hourly rate. Look at what you are being paid on an hourly basis. As long as you are aware of this, your quest should be to bring at least twice the value of that rate. This quest is another "de-commoditization" step for you. Business users have a generic term for this—ROI (Return on Investment). Make this your mantra for the rest of your career—your career is all about delivering the right ROI. Employ this skill consistently, and you will retain an increasing level of loyalty among all your clients. You will constantly be creating a business case for continued employment by your company and/or as a consultant for your clients.

I LOOKED

Today's date: / /

Think about all the people who are in your network. Can you connect two people (who don't know each other currently) who you think may establish a win-win relationship? This is one of the greatest gifts that you can give to both of those friends.

Planning:

By when will you connect these two people (date): / /

Who are they (names): 1. _____

2. _____

ACCOUNTABILITY REPORT

Find a friend who will help you to hold yourself accountable for this resolution. This is an important step. Please don't try to do it yourself. The process works great only if you enroll someone else to help you to be accountable. Now try to exceed the expectations. Share this with more than one person in your life. Your friend has to acknowledge that you have really done this.

S.No.   Date   Who did you connect?   What was the outcome?

1 _____

_____

2 _____

_____

Acknowledged By:

On Lasting Impressions

"Be more concerned with your character than your reputation, because your character is what you really are, while your reputation is merely what others think you are."

John Wooden

"On matters of style, swim with the current; on matters of principle, stand like a rock."

Thomas Jefferson

"Reputation is what men and women think of us; character is what God and angels know of us."

Thomas Paine

"Dance like no one is watching. Sing like no one is listening. Love like you've never been hurt and live like it's heaven on earth."

Mark Twain

"It's not the power, but the passion."

Tom Peters

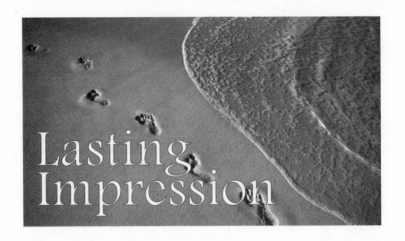

Lasting Impression

Your life is constantly reshaped by people you meet along the way. How many of your teachers do you remember from your school days? Probably only a few. Why not all of them? One good reason is that all of them did not make a lasting impression on you. Of all the teachers that you do remember, there may be one common thread—they gave their best to you. You can apply this to any kind of relationship (friends, co-workers, community members, project team mates and so on.) and the factor is the same—there are a few that will make a lasting impression and there are the rest. Our careers are no different and the same rules apply. We can adopt a simple rule when serving clients—give them our best: 110% of what we can, and watch miracles happen! What could we do in the next few engagements that will help us leave a lasting impression with your clients? Here are a few points to consider:

Care as if it's your own

I have talked to numerous customers about consultants who left a lasting impression on them. These consultants had one thing in common: they **cared**. They cared as if it was their own company or project, as if they had their personal money invested in the project or company. Every recommendation that was made by them had the best interest of the clients.

One of our consultants was working on a lengthy engagement at a customer location. He was so involved with the engagement and the client, that he knew more about the technology and the application than most people within the company. Meanwhile, there was a change in the leadership of the company and a new CEO came in. Needless to say, he noticed the great work of our consultant and was suitably impressed. During a discussion with the consultant's manager, the CEO was quite shocked to learn that this person was not an employee of his company. He could not believe that a consultant would care that much about an engagement. The consultant had indeed left a lasting impression.

Solve the right problems

Here is a classic consulting problem. Let's imagine a common consulting scenario. A company needs to automate a business process, and so it hires a consulting firm. The client's business manager describes the solution's features, and the consultants eagerly agree to produce that solution. In essence, the business manager's perceived solution becomes the consultants' understanding of the business need. These average (but technically sound) consultants may successfully deliver the requested solution, but the project may be doomed from the beginning. If the client's business manager proposed an ill-conceived solution, the project will fail and the real business need will remain unsatisfied. Consultants can easily fall into this trap and solve the wrong problem. People who make a lasting impression get to the bottom of the issues very quickly and are able to identify the "real" problem.

A few years ago, one of our star consultants on a client site was asked whether he was familiar with "Inbound Fax Integration." The manager had a budget allotted for the project and just wanted to confirm the effort estimates. The seasoned consultant began the project by asking a few detailed questions about the business need. The client really needed a simpler way for customers to order their products. Currently customers would order via fax. Someone had to feed in the fax orders into the system. The business manager had translated this into an Inbound Fax Integration project. Cutting a long story short, the consultant discovered that what they indeed required was an online ordering system. The inbound fax integration system was scrapped and he saved the client time and money. If you know how to solve the right problems for your clients, you will make a lasting impression during every engagement.

Get things done

Jim Rohn, noted personal development guru, says "there are either reasons or results." There are some people who will come up with phenomenal reasons (a.k.a. great excuses) for why things could not be done. Meanwhile, another group of people will produce results. The first group is forgotten quickly but second group makes a lasting impression. These consultants are masters of execution and they get things done.

The keyword is *dependable*. These consultants provide a sense of security and insurance on the engagements they are involved with. The client knows that these well-prepared consultants will warn them of possible issues, detect problems when they occur, and propose workaround strategies that keep the project moving forward.

Go beyond the call of duty

I was managing a Customer Relationship Management (CRM) project in Sunnyvale in late 1999. The client was an educational software provider that had multiple offices across the nation. The rollout plan was to take one office "live" at a time. When the east coast office went live, we added a significant number of concurrent users to the system and the system started "misbehaving." Once the first few hundred users had logged in, new users were unable to login. A SWAT team identified that the problem was in the database. We found that there were some processes on the server that were still hanging on even after the users were logged out.

We reported the problem to the database vendor and upgraded the system resources to tide through the interim. However, that would not solve the problem completely. One of the team members came up with an idea that we should identify and kill these orphan processes to ensure that the system resources would be released. This would be the stop gap arrangement until the database vendor solved the issue. It meant that some of us had to come in very early in the morning (around 5am) to monitor the system, to identify these orphan processes and kill them. Two team members volunteered to do this with me for the next few weeks. The problem was finally fixed with a patch from the database vendor, and we reverted to our normal schedules. These two team members are remembered even today by most of the project's stakeholders.

The deal is simple—recount any of your own projects. What do you remember? It's not those days when everything went as per the plan, nor those days when things went smoother than expected. Your vivid memories are when things went wrong or you were faced with some nasty surprises or system crashes. People vividly remember how they overcame adversity. If you want to make a lasting impression, you definitely should be a player during these adverse times. Consultants who patiently sit on the sidelines are quickly forgotten.

Be Resourceful

During one of the CRM implementations for a large bank in New York, I met a programmer who had just landed from Russia. His communication skills were a bit tough on us, (as he was just settling in) but his technical skills were excellent. I remember him even today because of the way he approached his work. Apart from being very thorough and dedicated, he always carried with him a CD library of all the re-usable code that he had collected over last twenty years. Granted, most of the code could not be used because the technologies were different. However, there were things that could easily be extended or slightly modified to suit the current scenarios. Obviously he was a very quick learner, and he had a great knack of using the resources that he had accumulated. Every now and then you find people who are resourceful in many different ways. Some know how to mine the web to find information; some have a great network of people with variety of skills; and some read voraciously, and are always up to date on what's happening. It's a pleasure to work with those people. You know that once a problem is handed off to them, they will find a way to solve them. Is it any wonder that these people are remembered for a long time?

Leave a legacy

When you join a company as a new-hire, most of you know that you are not going to stay in that company forever (until your retirement). There are exceptions, but I am talking about the general industry trend here. Leaving a legacy at your workplace is not easy. Think of all the people that worked with you in some of your past companies. How many people did you miss for more than a few months after they left or quit? There are not many people that come to mind. When I discuss this, people say that "nobody is indispensable," so how does one leave a legacy at work? I agree that nobody is indispensable, and I know it is hard to leave a legacy at your workplace. Come on, if it was easy wouldn't everyone be already doing it?

Have a Great Attitude

If leaving a legacy is in your mind, your attitude towards your job will be very different from when you treat your current job as a step towards your next job. Job skills are changing at a breathtaking pace and more companies are now truly "hiring for attitude, training for skills." What do you want to be remembered for? When you move on, your work still remains in the old workplace. Your memories still remain with the others you have left behind. How do you think they will remember you? This is based on several factors. Here are some questions to think about:

What was the measurable value that you added to the team and company while you were there?

How did you make others feel when you were around?

Were you there when you were needed?

Did you do what was needed or did you walk the extra mile?

On how many people's energizer list did your name appear?

What initiatives did you take on your own from concept to completion?

How easy were you to deal with? Were you a "low" maintenance person or a "high" maintenance person?

While you are still employed by your current company, start planning and executing an image that will be remembered for time to come. The key to remember is that the commodity crowd is easily forgotten.

MY LEGACY

Today's date: / /

Think about one initiative that you can take in the next one month that will elicit a "Wow!" experience from people around you.

Planning:

By when will you complete this task (date): / /

What do you plan to do?

_____

ACCOUNTABILITY REPORT

Find a friend who will help you to hold yourself accountable for this resolution. This is an important step. Please don't try to do it yourself. The process works great only if you enroll someone else to help you to be accountable. Now try to exceed the expectations. Share this with more than one person in your life. Your friend has to acknowledge that you have really done this.

S.No.	Date	What did you do?	What was the outcome?
1			
2			

Acknowledged By:

On Love

"Good enough never is."

Debbie Fields

"Do the best job and you'll never have any 'competition'."

Christopher Casey

"Not all things that count can be counted, not all things that can be counted count."

Albert Einstein

"There are no shortcuts to any place worth going."

Helen Keller

"There are two kinds of people, those that do the work and those that take the credit. Try to be in the first group, there is less competition there."

Indra Gandhi

A re you happy with your job?

The answer to this question is most often a "No" or a "Yes, but..." followed by a long explanation of why the person is unhappy. Listen some more, and the person will assure you that everything is right with him or her-only something or someone is screwing up, and he or she doesn't know what to do about it. However you slice it, the fact is harsh: most people are unhappy at work and aren't able to do a thing about it. Sad, indeed.

Most people think that if only just a few of those niggling problems were eliminated, presto!, their job would become more pleasant. The internal assumption for many of you would be to solve just those few problems; the internal assumption is that:

Being "Problem Free" = Happiness

If you are one of them, I have some news for you—you will always have problems in your job, and there is nobody who has eliminated all those problems. The good news, though, is that you don't have to eliminate all your problems to be happy in your job. In fact, how you approach those problems will determine your level of happiness. Even the world's wealthiest and most influential have problems, a revelation that surprises many. One can guess a person's place in the organization from the level and complexity of problems he or she is given to handle. In other words, you don't need to solve your problems to love your job. In fact, if you want to enrich your job, you need to ask for bigger problems and go after solving them.

Problems come so that heroes may overcome them.

Passion Rules!

Loving what you do is not just necessary but is a pre-requisite for success in your job. Nothing can substitute passion—not hard work, not intelligence! Do you love your job or not? Your answer to that question will shape your mood when you wake up and prepare for your workday. It will affect how you interact with your clients and co-workers. When you decide that you love your job, your mind will continually notice things that you love. If you decide that you don't love your job, you'll notice all the things that frustrate and irritate you. The choice is yours to make, and it will make a huge difference. What we should not forget is that it is a conscious choice we are making. A simple rule to remember is:

Success = Love what you do + Do what is required

Observe that there are two components on the right side of the equation. The temptation is to focus only on "Love what you do" and become stressed on all activities in the "Do what is required" category. The idea is to manage the required items, not eliminate them. In Silicon Valley, I get to meet other entrepreneurs and see the passion with which they build their companies. I have heard comments that entrepreneurs have this extra dose of passion because it is their company. I have the privilege of having been associated with many people before they decided to become entrepreneurs (while still employees at other companies), and I saw the same passion and drive in them even though they owned just a fraction of a percent of the company where they were employed. Ownership is seldom connected with passion, although ownership can help you justify your passion.

Who you are speaks so loudly that I can't hear what you say

When you love what you do, you don't have to announce it. People will feel the energy from within you. The output from your work will show the necessary evidence. Love has several desirable side effects.

> Ownership is seldom connected with passion, though it provides a reason to increase passion levels.

Productivity shoots up, as there is little room for negative energy. We attract positive people. Those who spread negative energy (pessimists) won't fetch enough support and will remain far. People will discuss ideas than discussing other people or events.

"Small minds discuss people, Average minds discuss events, and Great minds discuss ideas."

While this world could be a better place if everyone starts loving what they do, let's face the reality that we will be in a minority group if we love what we do. That means that there are many out there who will not share this passion and love, or worse yet, may have opposing views. The art is to co-exist with all sorts of people, but allow ourselves to be influenced by only a select few that will energize us. Start spreading the message in a small way about why you are excited about what you are doing, and perhaps you will connect a few people to your way of thinking. Just like loving what we do has positive side effects, not loving what we do has negative side effects. Most of our waking hours are at work, and how we feel at work carries through beyond work and to our home.

The "I Love my Job because..." exercise

Time and again I have seen people switch jobs thinking that the grass is greener on the other side, and once they move to the other job, they start looking at the brighter side of what they left.

When we are looking for a job, we tend to look at all the positives of a new job, and compare it with all the negatives of our current job. Naturally, the picture looks rosy and (as usual) provides the evidence supporting our decision to move on. It takes a while for us to settle down in our new job. Once settled in, we reverse the analysis. We notice the negatives of our current job and remember the positives of our past job. The remorse often hits hard, but then it's too late! Here is an exercise that ideally should be something that your company should get you to do. Anyway, we are not going to wait for that. Let us do that exercise ourselves.

I Love my job because... Identify and write down five reasons why you should love your job:

1. _____
2. _____
3. _____
4. _____
5. _____
Date: / /   Sign:_____

Take this exercise seriously. Here is why: your mind starts looking for evidence for some of the conclusions you make. By completing this exercise in all sincerity, you are planting some powerful seeds in your mind. Your mind will be working even when you are asleep to prove that your theories are right. You will be amazed at all the good things you will start to notice in your workplace, and in your job once you do this. Imagine doing this exercise in a group with your colleagues and each one of them comes up with their own list. If it is a closed group, you can share your thoughts with the other members of the group. Contrast and compare notes, and maybe you will notice some things that others notice that you didn't. There really may be more reasons than you listed to love your job.

Find a Mentor

There is a reason why I included finding a mentor in this chapter. It is interesting to note that most sports teams and individual sports persons have coaches, and they continue the coaching relationship even at the top of their career. However, consultants who have to play more than one game in their consulting careers (based on the nature of projects that they have to handle) don't seem to need a coach or a mentor. They hope to "figure it all out" on their own. Good coaches and mentors are hard to find. Find and engage with one or more mentors. Here's why: Work pressures are intense. Even if we have the best of intentions and do everything right, we may be shortchanged. The pressure itself won't break you; however, your response can affect both your mood and your performance. If you stay positive, you'll be able to resolve problems more quickly and more productively—easier said than done!

Old habits and patterns are hard to break, and we need help. If we tend to go with our standard response of finding faults at the workplace and with our job, we may not reach far. Good coaches look beyond your immediate situation and help you uncover the right questions about your work and your life. You will soon realize that asking the right questions is more important than getting the right answers. In order to start a new journey loving our life and our work, the shortcut may be to find a good mentor. That will be the best investment you would have made in yourself.

I LOVE MY JOB

Today's date: / /

Identify two people (preferably in your organization). Get together and complete the "I Love my job because ..." exercise. Share the results with each other. You may discover some new things to increase your love for your job.

Planning:

By when will you complete this task (date): / /

Who are the two people with whom you will work?
1._____ 2._____

ACCOUNTABILITY REPORT

Find a friend who will help you to hold yourself accountable for this resolution. This is an important step. Please don't try to do it yourself. The process works great only if you enroll someone else to help you to be accountable.

S.No.	Your friends	5 reasons why they love their jobs
1		
2		

Acknowledged By:

My Story

The difference between ordinary and extraordinary is that little "extra."

Jimmy Johnson

L et me start off by sharing two personal anecdotes that seem unrelated, but have served as turning points in my life. I began reading early in life, and I developed an insatiable desire to read every kind of book. I must have read close to 700 books by the time I was nine years old. When I was nine, I was fixated with this grand idea of writing a novel. I didn't tell this idea to anyone but simply began writing one. It took me about three months to complete a two hundred page novel.

When I announced that I had finished writing a novel, my parents were not only surprised but also concerned that there was something seriously wrong with me. They thought that I might need medical attention. My friends thought I had gone crazy. Other people—who knew that I read voraciously—thought that I had patiently copied from another book. None of this mattered to me. In my heart, I felt that I had written a good book, and I spent the next few months refining it. It helped a lot that I was also good at school. My parents thought that my novel-writing fixation would be a passing fad. As long as I did well in my studies, they didn't have to bother about these creative phases of my youth.

By the time I was ten, I was scouting around for a publisher. This was in the early 80s and we didn't have Internet and emails. I come from a middle class family that didn't have a phone, which was still a prized novelty granted by the government owned telephone department. The only option was to write to the publishers directly, pitching my novel. At ten, one is not really business savvy, and my lack of any formal business experience lent me creativity. So, I made up my own rules. Not surprisingly, I received about one response for every ten letters I sent—and that would be an incredulous No!

Months passed by, and I continued to pitch my story with no luck. In tandem, I even began writing my second novel. The response, or the lack of it, didn't bother me much. I put it down to a natural gestation process of the industry, and the thought of giving up didn't even occur to my decade-old wisdom.

After failing consistently in my strategy for two years, I changed my approach and decided to meet with the publishers in person. I convinced my parents to lend me money to travel, and started on my new adventure. The results were even worse. People thought it a big joke, when they saw me in flesh, and they were not to blame, considering I was a very wiry ten-year-old. Very rarely I would get someone to listen to my pitch seriously. The whole exercise was—ahem!—a big flop.

I changed my strategy once again. This time around, I wrote to other fiction writers to pitch my story, and that helped a bit. I got some responses that were mostly short missives wishing me luck in my endeavor. Three years had passed by now. I was thirteen and now had written four novels and there was no light in sight. Then something miraculous happened. One very famous writer of those times, G.Prakash, evinced interest in my work—and, more importantly, in the story of my travails. After many long letters through the snail mail, I was invited to spend a day with him in his home town. Prakash introduced me to one of his publishers who too liked my personal story more than my novel, and agreed to publish my work. Finally, after more than three years, I was published at the old age of thirteen. Everyone—including me—was surprised. I had become the youngest fiction writer of Karnataka state. This was in 1983.

Before I turned sixteen, six more of my books were published; I started working as a journalist for a local newspaper, and about a hundred articles and short stories were published in several magazines and newspapers across the state. Here are some of the lessons I learned from this whole exercise:

Pay the price to win the prize: If you believe in something and are willing to pay the price, you are sure to win the prize. Persistence pays—really.

Either you succeed or you learn: My three years of "failure" were a great investment in myself. I learnt some of the greatest business lessons before I had a serious need for them.

Focus long term: While pure luck or sheer coincidence (being at the right time at the right place) might give you a breakthrough sometimes, if you want serious results on any aspect of your life, you have to be willing and ready to take the long-term route.

Let me now switch gears and narrate how I became interested in building professional services teams. While journalism was exciting, it didn't meet my financial expectations. I scouted around for other fields that matched the creative intensity of writing.

In 1992 I took up a full-time job as a consultant with a financial software company, in their wholesale banking division. My core responsibility as a team member in the Foreign Exchange and Money Markets division (FX and MM) was to customize FX and MM programs to meet client needs. This was my first real full time job and it was exciting in that sense. In the eighteen months I spent at this company, my attempts to create a difference in the organization were insufficient, and I left in search of better, "ideal" places that would receive my "impact creating" resume with open arms.

In early 1994, I had a breakthrough. There was this CEO of a Malaysian conglomerate who had managed to look into time, and had realized that IT was going to be one sizeable weapon of strategic advantage he could wield in his market. I was given an opportunity to work for this company as a business analyst, analyzing basic needs and translating them into technology solutions. I was excited about the "promotion" and the opportunity to work in a foreign country. Fate, though, had other plans in store for me. I landed in Malaysia to find that the company ran only two software programs for its entire operations: Wordstar and

The author tries out a tri-cycle in Malaysia

Lotus 123. Two more programmers who were hired for the new company had already reported in. I spent the next two weeks talking with people throughout the company. I listened to people explain their needs, and then I created a shortlist of opportunities where new technology could fill these needs.

When I met with the CEO three weeks later, I was still under the impression that there was to be someone to manage the organization, not knowing that the CEO had no one in mind. Curiosity got the better of me, and I ventured to ask about the plans for the subsidiary. My CEO retorted that it was up to me to have a plan, rather than ask him for it. I suppose it was a defining moment in my life.

I realized that asking the right questions were as important, and perhaps even more important than finding the right answers. I spent the next two months educating myself about the business of computing, technology management, and business process reengineering. I presented a two year plan to the CEO, who simply said, "I like it." I was made the General Manager for the division.

The next two years were truly a test, since I had to work and learn simultaneously. What I learned I could apply almost instantly—how much better could an education get? Granted, I was not an expert, but I had the full support of an entire company to innovate and take risks. The two year project was extremely successful. Several Malaysian newspapers wrote articles about how we used technology to gain a competitive advantage in our business. I was also invited to share this story as a speaker at two international conferences in Singapore and Malaysia. Of course, I have lessons to share with you:

You have more capabilities than you can imagine: All you need is the right set of circumstances to bring out your true potential.

Larger expectations result in bigger results: If you expect great results from your employees, chances are they will produce them.

The next few years of my career involved managing technology projects in several countries. In 1997 my friend Mitesh Ashar, who was helping Silicon Valley companies recruit people, persuaded me to come to Silicon Valley so that I could rub shoulders with some of the most creative people in the world. I came to the U.S. reluctantly, but fell in love with the place and people. Subsequently, I was involved in growing and managing professional services teams at technologies like Vantive (acquired by PeopleSoft) and Broadvision. My teams had some of the best and brightest consultants from across the world. In the next three years I had ample opportunity to watch these consultants at close quarters; some really took off, while others simply withered away. Most consultants, though, were good—neither stars nor failures. They performed exactly to the levels expected of them.

Out of sheer curiosity, I began a closer observation of the consultants who out-performed the team. While at that, I also met up with other team leaders who managed different professional services divisions, and shared notes. "Who are your top performers and how did they reach there?" was my refrain, and I would make it a point to meet these performers. The war stories were rich in color, and I learned so many lessons from them.

In 2000 I joined hands with four bright folks I had met and started an IT services company called CIGNEX. We have been on a steady growth path and have added many extremely talented members who will help take this company to the next level. I have had an opportunity to put to use most of the learning from my writing and the Malaysian experience in this company.

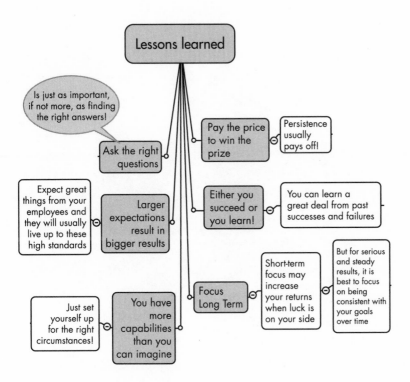

THE OUTER GAME

• Leverage • Like • Listen •Lead

On Leverage

"It marks a big step in a man's development when he comes to realize that others can be called in to help him do a better job than he can do alone."

Andrew Carnegie

"You can get everything in life you want if you will just help enough other people get what they want."

Zig Ziglar

"We must all hang together or most assuredly we shall hang separately."

Benjamin Franklin

"No individual can win a game by himself."

Pelé

T hese two words alone can change our entire life. If you manage to take away just these two words from my book, then I have achieved something. Time is the greatest equalizer. Everyone in this world—you, me, Bill Gates, the president of the United States, an aborigine in Australia, and that kindergartener—all have only twenty-four hours in a day: no more, no less. Time has no special treatment for anyone. No exceptions! However, we each achieve different results, simply because we invest our time and energy differently. What you make out of your twenty-four hours will be very different from what your neighbor or colleague will make out of it. There are many factors that determine this, such as effectiveness, productivity, time management skills, intellect, luck and so on. When you apply the concept of leverage in your life, you will be able to accomplish more in twenty-four hours than you can on your own. Every day, you have the opportunity to increase your leverageable assets. Most people think assets must be tangibles, such as cash, commodities, or real estate. However, I want to propose that some of your most valuable assets will be the strong relationships that you build throughout your lifetime and career. Imagine you had a friend whose knowledge and experience could guide you towards a solution to a problem on your current project. Their advice would be valuable to you, right? Well, many people don't think about relationships or even knowledge as assets, so they don't know how to leverage them.

Let's look at ways you can bring the power of leverage into your life. In the following exercise, you will get a status check and learn where you stand.

Last year's experience:
Number of clients you interacted with
Number of projects you worked on
Number of books that you read
Number of new acquaintances made
Number of active friends you had
Number of magazines you read
Number of seminars you attended
Number of educational TV programs that you watched
Number of interactions you had with your mentors

Close your eyes for a few seconds and think how many of the above activities really meant anything to you—enough that you applied some lessons from them in your life? Now expand this timeframe to include your experience since the time you were in college. Are you making the most of your leverageable assets and strengths? If you are not, you are like the majority of folks who add years to their experience but who are not going anywhere. There is no leverage whatsoever.

Let's say you have ten years of work experience. The key is to ask yourself whether you are bringing all your relevant experience from those ten years to work in your eleventh year. If you are, congratulations! If not, it's never too late to start.

Here are some thoughts on how to increase your leverage and move ahead.

Let go of the "Hulk Complex"

Take a moment to reflect on the following four statements. Which of them are true in your life?

1. I usually believe that I need to solve issues on my own.
2. I only ask for help when I have exhausted all my other options (and myself).
3. I am not very comfortable asking someone else for help.
4. I am most satisfied when I solve a problem without anyone else's help.

If your answer was true for two or more of the questions above, you have what is called as the Hulk Complex. Here's the news: whenever there is a problem, it only needs to be handled. There is **no** rule that it needs to be handled *solely* by you. That is a notion *you* have. Why do you think so? Let us look at some of your alternatives. Whenever you are presented with an issue, problem or a challenge, think for a moment if anyone else in your network has faced such a situation before. Call this person and ask the person questions, and listen to any advice they offer. No two business situations are exactly similar. However, there is enough to be learned from a similar experience. Now, if you don't know any such person in your network, look into your extended network for people whom your close friends might know. If they know someone who was in a dilemma similar to yours, get an introduction and talk to the other person. You may find a solution for your current situation, and you will also expand your network. Think of any other members in your professional associations or news groups that you belong to, who may have

> When you attempt to solve a problem all by yourself, you have only yourself as a resource. Is that enough?

solved this problem. Post a message to the group requesting help. If you can't find an answer through your network, your next step is to research the problem. Go to a library or bookstore; research the topic on the web; and look through your archives for relevant journal and magazine articles. An author's bibliography can often point you to other great sources.

I can go on, but you get the idea. When you attempt to solve a problem all by yourself, you have only YOURSELF as a resource. When you start reaching out to your network, you are leveraging something more powerful than yourself—your network's combined resources. Know this: our true power comes from *solving* the problem, not attempting to solve it ourselves. If leveraging our network will let us solve the problem better and faster, it would be foolish not to do so.

The benefits of this exercise are enormous. Even if we already possess the best solution, we get an opportunity to hear multiple perspectives from other sources. If we consistently engage in this form of an exercise, you will notice that your level of thinking goes up. Also, since most of the folks ask us back a variety of questions, we soon start asking those questions ourselves before seeking advice.

Be gracious when using leverage

A business relationship is like a lever; it can help you achieve more than you could on your own. However, if you put too much stress on a relationship, it will snap just like a lever. Just because you have an urgent problem doesn't mean that your friend will have the knowledge or the time to help you. If they can't help you, then politely ask if they know someone who might have the necessary knowledge or time. If not, thank them and be sure to close your interaction with them positively. Don't end the conversation on a sour note! Also, if someone helps you, in any way, be sure to thank them. Let them know how much their help means to you.

Give first

The golden rule is that you should adopt a genuine "giving"

mindset. Again, we cannot fake it; people can see through it early.

Here is a status check for you: List at least ten people who can "Leverage" your time, talent, skills or network. Who can draw upon your leverageable assets to help them solve their problems?

1. _____   6. _____

2. _____   7. _____

3. _____   8. _____

4. _____   9. _____

5. _____   10. _____

If you can't come up with at least ten names quickly, check your "Giving Index" and fine tune it. As the word itself means it, "leverage" is two-sided. If you need to approach someone for some help, they must be able to receive something out of giving you the help. In effect, what do you have for them?

Points of Leverage

Know and use your leverage points: "leverage what?" is a commonly asked question whenever I talk about this subject. Here are some pointers that may get you thinking.

People: People are the biggest leverage points. Here are some categories of people to look at:

Our colleagues

Our ex-colleagues

Our classmates from schools & colleges

Alumni association members

Teachers from business schools

Friends

Members from professional associations that we may belong to

Employees from our partner companies

Employees from our vendor companies

Friends from volunteer organizations that we may belong to.

People who attended conferences or seminars with us.

People are a two-way street. If we want to get value from

anyone, we should be willing and have the capability to add value back to him or her.

Books: I read one book a week and this has helped me tremendously. My routine has become easy with the audio book revolution and the iPod. Again, there is an information overload, and picking the right books to read is a big challenge. Here are some thoughts:

Ask your mentors and coaches for their book recommendations

Read book summaries: if you like what you read, you can invest on reading the full book.

Learn what the top performers are reading now.

Search for bibliography in good books.

Look for book recommendations and reveiws in magazines that you respect.

Blogs: Blogs form one the best parts of the web. Susan Ward, an expert on this topic, defines a good blog as "a regularly updated online journal of information and opinions." Experts in various fields have either set up or are setting up blogs. Not only should you identify a set of blogs that you should visit often, you should seriously consider setting up your own blog, discussing ideas and opinions in your areas of expertise. By choosing the right blogs to read, you are making an investment in your personal brand. Both these investments have huge payoffs but don't expect returns on day one! To get into the blogworld quickly, check out blogrolls of people you respect.

Magazines: Pick any topic and you will find a ton of magazines. Don't let the sheer numbers overwhelm you. Pick a few good magazines and read them regularly: consistency and discipline are the keys. Explore whether you can contribute articles to one or more magazines.

Newsletters: Many newsletters have been reduced to marketing brochures. However, there are many newsletters in every field that offer rich information every week. Create email folders, and if you use Outlook, you can setup rules to send these newsletters directly to the designated folders. You can check and read them at your convenience.

Events: Industry events, panel discussions, conferences, seminars, or workshops have multiple benefits. (Interestingly, most of these events happen outside working hours.) You not only gain valuable insights, but events provide a great way to network with conference and workshops speakers, like-minded professionals and media folks.

Your work: Your day-to-day work can be a great leverage point if approached in the right fashion; most professionals treat each project and assignment as a series of tasks and just work towards generating output at required quality levels. It is easy to miss the forest for the trees here. Every disciplined effort has multiple rewards. When you are engaged in a project, ask some of the following questions to unravel the hidden leverage points:

Will this be useful for any of our other customers? (reusability)

Can we make a case study out of this? (Marketing)

Can I create a white paper based as this work? (Marketing)

Can I create a presentation about this for my team members or others within the company? (Personal brand building)

Is this project worth adding to my resume? (Building experience)

Can I write an article in a trade journal about the technology or the project? (Personal brand building)

Is anything that I learnt here useful to anybody in my network? (Personal brand building)

Work becomes more enriching if you can extract higher leverage from it for yourself and your company.

Your hobbies and interests: This is the most underused leverage point. Since your hobbies and interests may not be connected to your work, it is alright to assume that you should not mix the two. However, there are many ways you can leverage this. Hobbies and special interests are great for building rapport with people having similar interests. You and another coworker can build an instant rapport by simply picking up a game and playing it together. You have an audience at work that may be willing to support you for developing your other talents. You have a few more ways of growing and expanding your network. There may be professional associations or clubs where you may meet other interesting people.

Websites: We all know that there are thousands out there and there are a few that may help you personally and professionally. My friend Munwar Shariff (one of the cofounders of Cignex) has a single page (his home page), where all the links to his favorite websites are neatly categorized and organized. This home page acts as a launch pad for his browsing activities. One of my other friends is a power user of the Yahoo! Toolbar and has every important website that he visits bookmarked under proper categories on the toolbar. You can use any of such techniques or develop one of your own to build up your browsing skills.

Videos: My team and I have benefited hugely from video training programs on topics like leadership, team building, and strategy. Watching a video training session in groups helps you and the group get the most out of it. We watch a video segment every week for about thirty minutes, and then sit around the table where everyone would share what they got out of the segment and how (if) they plan to use it in their lives in the next few days. We not only learn from the video but also get to hear everyone's perspectives on the same thirty minute segment.

Google Answers: Google has not paid me to do this but I do want to shamelessly promote this wonderful service. The concept is simple. You post your question on the Google Answers website and attach a price tag to the answer (let's say $25 for one of your questions). Your question will be picked up by one of the prescreened researchers and he or she will provide an answer in a few hours or days. If you are satisfied with the answer your money will be paid to the researcher. You will be amazed at the quality of answers that you can get. It is almost like hiring some of the best brains in the world for a song.

Give it a try. The temptation would be to save money as most of this information is available on the net in some website or the other. Look, either you save money or save time. I would sincerely urge you to pick the latter, as money can be earned back, but you can't get back time!

Social Networking: There is so much buzz about social networking and I really don't know which of the services will emerge winners. I prefer "LinkedIn" (www.linkedin.com). Social networking is nothing but an implementation of "six degrees of separation" on the Internet. Once you become attached to a social networking service, you will be amazed at how many people you can reach through your own set of contacts. One caveat: use this with care.

I LEVERAGE

Today's date: / /

We went through the points of leverage in this chapter. Whenever I have asked people to do this exercise, they always tell me that they discovered that they had more resources to leverage than they previously thought. Take a notebook and start identifying your points of leverage. The chapter highlighted some of the points of leverage and you can use them as your starting points. You can also add your own categories.

Planning:

By when will you connect this exercise (date): / /

Who will you share it with (names):_____

ACCOUNTABILITY REPORT

Find a friend who will help you hold you accountable for this resolution. This is an important step. Please don't try to do it yourself. The process works great only if you enroll someone else to help you be accountable. Share your points of leverage with your trusted friend. Discuss how you plan to leverage your resources in the next few weeks.

Acknowledged By:

On Likeability

"And in the end, it's not the years in your life that count. It's the life in your years."

Abraham Lincoln

"If you don't like something, change it. If you can't change it, change your attitude. Don't complain."

Maya Angelou

"Friend: One who knows all about you and loves you just the same."

Elbert Hubbard

"Friends are those rare people who ask how we are and then wait to hear the answer."

Ed Cunningham

Likeability

n life, we all meet two kinds of people:

Energizers: people who make us feel good when we are with them. They boost our energy level.

Dissipaters: people who drain our energy and reduce our drive. We can't explain the feeling but it's certainly frustrating. Stop for a second and fill out the initials of people for both the categories.

Energizers	Dissipaters
1. _____	1. _____
2. _____	2. _____
3. _____	3. _____
4. _____	4. _____
5. _____	5. _____
6. _____	6. _____
7. _____	7. _____
8. _____	8. _____
9. _____	9. _____
10. _____	10. _____

Here is another challenge. Can you identify at least twenty people who you think will put you in their energizer list?

People who will put you on their energizer list:

1. _____	11. _____
2. _____	12. _____
3. _____	13 _____
4. _____	14. _____
5. _____	15. _____
6. _____	16. _____
7. _____	17. _____
8. _____	18. _____
9. _____	19. _____
10. _____	20. _____

Most people (if they are honest) have trouble completing the above list in less than ten minutes. For argument sake let us call this our "Likeability Index." The goal for us is to look for ways to increase our likeability index-at least double it. Here are some thoughts for increasing your likeability index.

Make others feel good about themselves

Imagine that you have lunch with someone you know. Perhaps it is a coworker, client, partner, friend, or family member. You chat during lunch, but afterwards you each have different things you need to do. Think for a second what goes on in the other person's mind right after your meeting. How does this person feel about himself or herself? Up or down? Better than before he met you or worse? Positive or negative? Optimistic or pessimistic? What did you desire to engender in this person? What are two things that you want this person to remember about the meeting? How you make another person feel about himself or herself is the biggest factor in determining whether you are likeable to that person or not.

Most often, people tend to talk about themselves and want to make a good impression. I have some news. Nobody in this world will care more about you than they would care about themselves. Believe me, if you make them feel good about themselves, you will get a chance to tell your story. For now, let us focus on the other person. Our turn will come, sooner than we think is possible.

Be genuinely interested in other people

There is a saying that you have to fake it before you make it. Unfortunately, that won't work when it comes to people and relationships. Remember that this is a busy world and people have less time to share with others-many of us are multitasking all the time. Have you seen people simultaneously talking on the phone, typing an email and also listening to some dialogue on the side? If you are one of those who build relationships while working on something else on the side (optimizing your time probably) you will not get far. It is easy for people to realize that they are not on your priority list. People watch your actions, behaviors, questions, and responses. They want to know where your attention is focused. If you pretend to be interested in people, it will harm you more than it will help you.

People can take criticism and even rejection, but very few people tolerate indifference. Being indifferent is the most brutal attack imaginable on another person. People want to be genuinely valued and cared for. When we do that, the same feeling is reciprocated (mostly). If we are artificial or deceitful, people will figure that out soon. So, don't play games with people!

Add measurable value

Every interaction between two people provides an opportunity for value exchange. Your key objective should be to add measurable value to the other person. The basic requirement then, is to find out what the other person values most. Take time to learn the other person's interests. What does the person dream about or aspire towards? What does he or she yearn to become? What is the roadmap he or she has crafted for the next few years? Over a span of few months or few years, if WE helped the other person reach dreams or aspirations earlier than he or she planned to reach there, we have given a gift that very few people can give. It is the gift of TIME. Because of your gift, the person now has more time to pursue additional goals.

These interactions can happen only if we have developed a trusting relationship with the other person. People don't reveal their deepest fears, hopes, dreams, and aspirations to strangers.

Develop a healthy self-esteem

How you feel about yourself will play a major role in how you interact with the rest of the world. If you feel that you are worth nothing, then you will not be open to leverage by other people. This will make it hard for you gain leverage through other people. You may feel guilty about just getting something without being able to give in return. The power of reciprocation is immense. When you can't reciprocate well, you also tend not to RECEIVE. You can miss out big time if you don't have a healthy self-esteem in place. The other key factor to note is that a low self-esteem can indicate that you don't love or like yourself. If that is the case, how can you expect others to like you?

Find Similarity

People like to be with others similar to themselves in some respects. If you are smart enough to figure out similarities between you and the other person in the first few minutes of the conversation, you have a good chance to be likeable. Here are some areas to start thinking:

FOCUS	COMMENTS
1. Common People	Do you both know anybody in common? Can you refer to some experiences with these common friends?
2. Education	Did you both study at the same college, same geography, same discipline, same times?
3. Job Functions	Are your roles, duties or responsibilities similar?
4. Common interests	Do any of your hobbies, interests, passion match up?
5. Common associations	Do you belong to some similar professional associations, clubs or charity
6. Common role models	Are you fans of the same role model(s)

7. Common objects	Do you own the same car, watch, boat, computer etc.
8. Common beliefs	Do you have the same belief system, religious or otherwise?
9. Common goals	Are you both working towards similar but complementary goals

The above list is just to aid you in your rapport building exercise. You may have others that you can easily add to your list. Think about them and customize the list to suit your needs.

Be trustworthy

People who trust each other will share all kinds of information. If you are close to someone, then you will know a lot more information about this person than what the general public will know. Much of this information was shared with you with an implicit agreement that you would never misuse it. The surest way to lose someone's trust is to use privileged information to your personal gain or advantage (there are many more ways to lose trust but this one makes it faster too). Possessing privileged information presents shortcuts to gain personal advantages from time to time, but we should resist the temptation to take these shortcuts. Here's a quick test: Think of someone whom you like a lot, but is not trustworthy. Do you draw a blank? Most certainly!

Be optimistic

We all like to be around people who bring life and fresh air to the party. I am not saying that if you are a pessimist you won't be liked. In fact, you may be liked a lot (by other pessimists). You can only imagine what a bunch of pessimists say when they get together (remember, pessimists never call themselves pessimists, most often, the term they use will be something like "practical," "realistic," or something else). The key to **positive thinking** is to hope for the best, *and* to be prepared for the worst! Deep down in our hearts, we all want to grow and move up. Be a spark that will light the fire in someone and move him or her towards their goals. You will not only be liked, you will also be remembered for injecting the fuel of positive energy.

MY LIKEABILITY

Today's date: / /

Find two people who you think like you. Your objective is to have a one-to-one meeting with them in the next seven days and find out at least three reasons why they like you.

Planning:

By when will you connect this exercise (date): / /

Who will you share it with (names):

1. _____

2. _____

ACCOUNTABILITY REPORT

Find a friend who will help you to hold yourself accountable for this resolution. This is an important step. Please don't try to do it yourself. The process works great only if you enroll someone else to help you to be accountable. Write down everything that you learn from these one-to-one meetings. Did you learn anything new about yourself?

Acknowledged By:

On Listening

"You'll never know how close you are to a million-dollar idea unless you're willing to listen."

John Maxwell

"Big people monopolize the listening, small people monopolize the talking."

David Schwartz

"It's better to keep your mouth shut and give the impression that you're stupid than to open it and remove all doubt."

Rami Belson

"There is nothing so annoying as having two people talking when you're busy interrupting."

Mark Twain

"Wise men talk because they have something to say; fools, because they have to say something."

Plato

L isten

No one will dispute that listening is more important than talking in communication. However, the same people also agree that listening is one of the biggest problem areas in communication. I am baffled by people's temptation to talk and dominate every conversation when all of us know that listening is more important than talking. A wise man once said, "there is a reason why we are given two ears and one mouth." A few reasons why most people focus on talking rather than listening:

Ego: You feel you are the most important person, and you can show it to others only by talking. In fact you may be wondering, "If I don't talk about myself or my accomplishments, how will I ever claim the respect that I truly deserve. How will people know otherwise?"

Lack of knowledge of asking questions: When you don't know how to ask the right questions, your comfort zone will be in talking about whatever you know, even if it hardly makes any sense to the other party.

You can't handle silence: Sometimes silence is required, and a pause is quite all right. People need time to process whatever they hear. If you can't handle silence, you start talking to fill the void.

Feeling incomplete: You must tell everything, else you feel incomplete.

Unused brain capacity: It is said that listening requires lesser use of the brain's capacity than talking. Maybe that's why most people keep thinking about what they should say next, rather than listening to the other person. There is a saying "feedback is the breakfast of champions." There is no feedback if there is no listening. If you want to be a champion, start listening. Here are some ways to improve your listening ability:

Listen to yourself first

People have different names for this activity. In some contexts it is called plain thinking. In this fast paced world, the norm has been "Ready, Fire, Aim!" Thinking will bring it back to a saner, "Ready, Aim, Fire!" A variation to this is also called "intuition" or "listening to your gut." We should know what this is and start taking advantage of it.

We need to listen to our self-talk. There is a constant chatter in our mind. Psychologists say that every day tens of thousands of thoughts pass through our mind. Interestingly, most of the thoughts that pass through our mind today are the same ones that went through us yesterday, the day before, last month, or even last year. It's like a record being played over and over when the needle is stuck. We can stop this monotony if we start taking conscious control of our thoughts. Start listening to what you are saying to yourself at moments of joy, sorrow, frustration and so on. You will be amazed at what you will find out. Most people have so much of negative "self-talk" that it is unbelievable. If you think about what you are trying to achieve from all this negative self-talk, you will realize that it is nothing much.

A major part of your self-talk will be related to what I call the "Poor Me!" syndrome. This is the inner attempt to convince yourself that nothing is ever your fault, it's all beyond your control. Other people and circumstances prevent your from achieving your goal or reaching happiness. It's very easy to fall into this trap and blame forces outside your control. So, when you notice the "Poor Me!" syndrome inside your head, put a stop to the negative self-talk.

On the positive side, you need to encourage positive self-talk. Catch yourself when you engage with yourself in positive self-talk. Take full accountability for your self-talk today. Nobody can listen to your self-talk. Only you can!

Listen for Insights

People enjoy it when you listen to them. By listening carefully to what they say, we can understand the person's values and priorities. The key is not to pass judgment, either openly or in our mind while the other person is talking. A person's values, beliefs and priorities are not typically announced or publicly shared. Unless we are close to a person and have a long-standing trusting relationship with him or her, we may not get to hear these kinds of information. Listening with care will reveal this information over a period of time.

When you listen, you will gain invaluable insights into a person's values, beliefs, and priorities. Again, you will be one of the few people in the person's life who possess this very personal knowledge.

Ask the right questions

Our ability to talk less and listen more will greatly depend on two things: 1. Our wanting to listen, and 2. Our ability to ask the right questions. Closed-ended questions are those that will elicit short answers such as a "yes," a "no," an "OK," or a "maybe." These closed-ended questions do not invite the other person to talk, so we will not be able to listen. In a project situation, here are some good starting questions to ask people:

1. What are some of the problems that you are trying to solve by implementing this solution? (You will learn some of the key objectives of the project.)

2. I'm curious to know how you arrived at picking this product (these products) as choice implementation vehicles? (You will find out what features are important) What were some of the features that you liked in these products? (You will uncover their interest in the selected products.)

3. Would you mind explaining how this project fits into the overall puzzle? (You will invite a big-picture discussion.)

4. What is the roadmap for the next few years for this project? (You can learn about the long-term vision for this

project.) Who are the people being impacted?

5. How do people do their jobs right now? (You will see the scope and breadth better.)

Of course, you are the best judge in determining what are the best open-ended questions for a particular situation. You will have to practice, though. Here is an exercise to jog your brain: Identify five open-ended questions that you can ask at the next meeting you plan to attend. Write what you hope to learn from each of the responses:

Question 1: _____

What I hope to learn: _____

Question 2: _____

What I hope to learn: _____

Question 3: _____

What I hope to learn: _____

Question 4: _____

What I hope to learn: _____

Question 5: _____

What I hope to learn: _____

Get fast feedback

Receiving feedback about ourselves and our work is extremely important. Here are three questions that you can ask to get the right feedback:

What am I doing well that I should continue to do?

What am I doing that I should stop doing?

What am I not doing that I should start doing?

Implement a feedback analysis loop

I first learned about this concept from the legendary management guru Peter Drucker. The origin, I believe is from a

14th century German theologian. The concept is simple, but it will work only if followed consistently over a long period of time:

Record a significant decision you intend to make and your expected ideal outcome as a consequence of that decision. Record the actual outcome for each decision as and when it occurs. You will soon realize that it will be impossible for you to succeed in all your decisions. The actual outcomes do not match the desired outcomes. What has not changed with time is that sometimes we win and sometimes we lose. There are no guarantees.

If you refer back to this logbook after about twelve months and analyze your decisions and outcomes, you will learn about your strengths. You will know those decisions you can make very well and those that you need help with. You want to be good at your decision making ability, because your decisions will shape your destiny.

Listen without prejudice

Good inputs can come from anywhere. When you listen, drop all prejudices that you may have about the person who delivers the message. It's easy to put people into a box and tune out their messages. Generalizations about people: "He is smart," "She is creative," "He is a loser," are our ways of simplifying inputs from a particular person, our way of eliminating noise from the signal. Here are some thoughts to handle this situation:

Attach the message to a credible source: Whoever gives you the message, treat it as if one of your mentors gave you that message. You will now treat the message with a different level of respect than before.

Resist the temptation to reach conclusions instantly: This is another mind trick. We are wired to conclude quickly. This is our way of checking off an item in our "to do" list. By not having to conclude anything instantly, you will be forced to fetch more inputs on the idea rather than dissecting it on the spot with incomplete information. Remember, our mind starts looking for evidence to make conclusions.

Keep an open mind: You never know where the next big idea is hidden, or who will give it to you. If you close your minds, you will miss something, and may not even know what you missed or that you missed something.

I LISTENED

Today's date: / /

Implement feedback analysis loop for the next 30 days. Whenever you decide something significant, write down the decision and the expected outcome because of that decision.

ACCOUNTABILITY REPORT

Find a friend who will help you hold you accountable for this resolution. This is an important step. Please don't try to do it yourself. The process works great only if you enroll someone else to help you to be accountable.

What do you learn about your decision-making capabilities? Thirty days is a short timeframe to maximize the benefits of the feedback analysis loop. If you are completely happy with the results you are getting from the decisions you are making, you can stop implementing the feedback analysis loop, otherwise, continue the wonderful journey you have already begun.

Acknowledged By:

On Leading

"Outstanding leaders go out of their way to boost the self-esteem of their personnel. If people believe in themselves, it's amazing what they can accomplish."

Sam Walton

"If a man hasn't found anything to die for, he isn't fit to live."

Dr. Martin Luther King Jr.

"A leader is one who sees more than others see, who sees farther than others see, and who sees before others see."

Leroy Eimes

"Leadership is the capacity to transform vision into reality."

Warren Bennis

"Nearly all men can stand adversity, but if you want to test a man's character, give him power."

Abraham Lincoln

LEAD

I heard this amazing story from noted leadership guru, Gerry Faust.

One early morning, four people meet in a park. None of them know each other, but at that time of the day and looking at the way all of them were dressed, it is easy to guess that they are going to take a morning walk in the park. They introduce themselves, and go through the ritual small talk covering weather, stock and politics—sharing no personal information. As the conversation proceeds, the four become more comfortable with each other. Since all of them share the same purpose, they decide that they would hike up the mountain trail. Thus starts the journey.

As they start walking, the small talk progresses towards personal discussions, and all four begin sharing information about their work, family, and so on. The walk gets along fine; the weather is good and the conversations make this all the more interesting. The path up the mountain narrows as they walk up.

There is a mountain on one side of the path and a deep valley on the other side; trees of all sizes dot the place. They turn a corner and are stopped by a large boulder blocking their path. There is pitch silence for a few seconds, as the four don't know how to respond to that situation. Unless they move the rock, there is no way they could proceed with their hike. Something interesting happens at that moment. One of the four rolls up his sleeves and says, "Come on guys, let's move the rock and clear the way."" He means every word he says, and you could see the conviction on his face. Also, the tone and the style suggests that he is not asking for opinions: it looks like he makes a decision for the group.

The other three look at each other. The responses from the trio vary. One says, "I don't think it is worth our time. May be we should just head back the trail." The second person says, "It may not be hard to move this rock, but what is the plan? Let me know what I should do to help." The last one says, "We have to be careful, guys. There may be people hiking down in the valley. We might kill someone if we are not careful."

The rest of the story is not relevant here, but the point to remember is that the rock was the defining moment for demonstration of leadership. Without that rock obstructing the team's goal, no leader would have emerged. Rocks help. Look at all the rocks in your business. Customers, for sure, can provide us with many rocks. Their projects and their issues provide a great opportunity to demonstrate leadership.

What other rocks do we see in our business and personal life? Every rock will provide us with an opportunity to shine as a leader. If you observe the story, there was no committee, nor there was any vote to choose a leader to take the initiative to move the rock. Leadership just happened. Anybody could have assumed that role at that moment. Still, only one picked up the opportunity to do so. Look at your past at your workplace and into your life. Did you miss any such opportunity when facing a rock where you could have emerged as a leader? How can you ensure that you don't miss any other such opportunities in the future? Can you identify the rocks that might show up in the next few weeks so that you are ready?

Leadership is not tied to position

Many people say that they have very little control over what they do and what value they can bring to the table because most of their actions are determined by their bosses (people in power positions). They just have to follow orders, so what creativity would they bring to the mix? It's almost as if they were saying, "If only I was in that position, things would have been different. But..."

The trap is so subtle that we don't even realize that we are in it. But once we are caught in it, it swallows our confidence very easily. Remember, once we have concluded that we can't do anything significant without formal power and authority, we have given yourself permission NOT to do anything exceptional. Worse yet, we are also NOT accountable for our performance because we are HELPLESS. We have many reasons for this problem but the reason is never OURSELVES! Do you realize how dangerous this can be?

We should realize that we don't need a lot of creativity to move up, if we have unlimited time, money and resources. Our test of creativity is when we are within a box, limited by constraints (time, money, power, resources), and we still have to win. When I moved to Silicon Valley in 1997, I witnessed the bubble first hand. Companies were buying software and services whether they needed them or not. Venture capitalists were furious if portfolio companies didn't hire fast or spend millions on marketing. "Eyeballs" were one of the key performance indicators. Revenue and profitability were the last things that were discussed in the boardroom. We have since then corrected ourselves, and are back to ground reality now. What was required to succeed then is very different from what we need to succeed now. We have no option and no excuses but to lead an initiative, movement, or crusade and take it from concept to completion. Knowing all our constraints and being creative in working around them is the only way out. Don't wait for the ideal day when you would have no constraints on your capability. That day will never come.

Be what you want to become

One of the biggest misconceptions is this: we feel that if we work very, very hard and excel in our current positions, we should rightly be promoted to the next position. It's almost like a reward, if you will, that we expect for doing the job very well. This is what I call the "Entitlement Mentality," and it should be nipped in the bud. The reward may be received sometimes, but treating it like a formula or rule would be foolish. If you want to earn a promotion quickly, learn what skills you will need in the next position. Acquire and demonstrate these skills in your current position. In other words, you should already be acting as if you were already promoted, before you are handed that position.

Here is an example: If you are a team member and are interested in moving up to be a team leader, volunteer to do some of the following tasks a team leader may be doing today:

- Prepare weekly status reports
- Manage issues
- Prepare project plans
- Prepare meeting minutes every time there is a significant meeting

You can call this approach by many different names—going beyond the call of duty, walking the extra mile, being proactive, or whatever name you choose—but DO it. Set a goal to BE today whatever you want to become. Don't wait to be handed a position and fully trained. Show initiative. You first BE, and then you GET!

Fill in the blanks

Any organization will have gaps. Some of them have gaps of the size of a teacup and some the size of the Grand Canyon. These gaps are blanks, just waiting for someone to fill them. Do you know of any blanks in your organization that you can fill? Leading is as simple as filling in the blanks.

The leadership litmus test is our ability to pick the right blanks to fill. Once we identify the blanks, how do we know they are the right ones for us to fill? The keyword here is "relevant." The question to ask ourselves is that if we fill this blank, will it raise the bar for us, our team and/or our organization? If yes, one should go all out and start filling in the blanks. Here is an example of leadership that I vividly remember:

The Find an Expert project: A few years ago there was a small team of people who were interested in building an intranet for their whole group. There were many other priorities for the group. Although the intranet was important, it was not an urgent priority. Nevertheless, the group managed to bring out the first version of the intranet in less than a month, using their night and weekend leisure time. Like many intranet projects, it was easy to create but very hard to get people to adopt it.

The initial version included an address book, a document reporting system and an ability to share solutions to commonly-faced problems in the field. The intranet did not take off. There was little support from anyone in the company and not many people even visited it. The biggest problem was that this intranet had no "killer" application that would bring back visitors again and again. The team tenaciously continued to refine the intranet in their spare time. They knew that if they continued to involve users and bring relevant features into the mix, they could ultimately win. A few months later they created an application called "Find an Expert" that brought the much sought attention to the intranet. The concept was simple. They created a three level database that defined all the required and relevant technical skills. Here is a sample entry from the skill-set database:

Level 1	Level 2	Level 3
Database	Oracle	Stored procedures
	Oracle	SQL / DBA
	Oracle	Performance tuning

Every team member on the field had to fill a self-service form; rating him or herself on all the skills they processed, on a scale of one to six (one being novice, and six being guru). In less than two weeks, we had hundreds of consultants and their skill sets in a searchable database.

The other module was a web based interface to "Find an Expert." With this feature, any consultant could search for experts in a particular skill set. Suppose a consultant had a question related to Oracle performance tuning, all he had to do was go to the "Find an Expert" page and search for experts on this topic. The query would return all the people who had rated themselves on this skill, with gurus leading on the top. The result set also included every guru's contact information. With just a click, a consultant could touch base with an expert and quickly solve the problem. This feature was an instant hit and was the tipping point in adopting intranet. Suddenly, everyone was talking about Guru—the rebranded intranet application. It provided the entire company a much needed competitive advantage.

The team won the accolades it truly deserved. It took a lot of hard work, and there was no quick success. "Find an Expert" was not even a feature that was conceived in the beginning. The team truly wanted to make a difference: to fill in the blanks. Yet, when it started, the intranet appeared to fill a low importance blank. The team spent a lot of time listening to people explain their needs, and they then built a system that filled an important blank. This one example embodies leading, learning and listening; and the team adapted their project to fill an important blank for the entire company.

Be ready for your leadership moments

Tony Robbins said "Luck is the meeting point of opportunities that are passing by and your awareness in grabbing them." We can get luckier by being ready to pay the price to win the prize.

Leadership moments come to all of us. However, only people who are ready to capitalize on them will emerge as leaders. This book, and many others, deals with several fundamental leadership qualities that you can develop on your own. They work for people across all disciplines.

I came across one such leadership moment, and even today I feel fortunate to have used it wisely. My history in the Valley began as a consultant, recruited by a large firm managing a project for a big bank. I was told that the golden path was to come in as a consultant, prove my technical expertise, bide my time, and then move up. The U.S. experience counted more than anything else. Thus began my U.S. career.

While I was settling in, I also trained in a leading CRM application. I was then involved in some in-house projects, fine-tuning my technical skills. Meanwhile, the company was concluding a worldwide CRM implementation for a large PC manufacturer. The company needed someone to create a worldwide implementation roadmap, a sort of cookbook for rolling out the solution across the world. It was a six week project for one person, and my project head asked if I would be interested. The project had very little technology involvement, and other team members were shying away from taking it up, fearing it wouldn't add to their resume skills. I took it up, and today I am glad I did. It gave me an opportunity to meet the brains behind the multimillion dollar CRM implementation up close and at very personal levels. I got to meet the entire team—designers, developers, project managers, user representatives, subject matter experts, and documentation folks—almost everyone who plays a key role in the implementation. I didn't have a precedence set to work with. There was no "similar" document to refer to. Honestly, I had an opportunity to set the standards and benchmark for any future documenting that the group would engender. Six weeks later, I delivered a one-hundred page cookbook.

The client received the document very well, and I was no longer just another consultant. I had "de-commoditized" myself with a six week, non-technical engagement. When I picked this assignment up, I had no idea it could vault my career upwards.

Be on the lookout for leadership moments. They can come in various forms and shapes. Most often, they come dressed in overalls—dirty, baggy ones at that. Look for opportunities that other people are not willing to take up, the tendency is to do what others do. Rarely do people want to travel the road less traveled.

I LEAD

Today's date: / /

Tap into at least two leaders whom you admire (in your company or outside) and schedule a one-on-one meeting with them. Your objective is to find out what the leadership moments were in their lives. What made them leaders? Deadline: 30 days from now.

Planning:
By when will you complete this exercise: / /
Who are the people that you will tap into:

1. _____

2. _____

ACCOUNTABILITY REPORT

Find a friend who will help you hold you accountable for this resolution. This is an important step. Please don't try to do it yourself. The process works great only if you enroll someone else to help you to be accountable.

What did you learn from these two leaders that you can apply in your own life?

Acknowledged By:

what *next* ?

Congratulations! You have read the book completely. You are among the minority that actually complete reading a business book. However, this is not a destination but a start of a new journey. My friend jokingly says, "Knowing is not doing, but doing is doing." You know a lot, but none of that will mean anything if you don't act on anything that you learned. Here are some of my thoughts on what you can do next.

Take action

Appropriate enough, and I am sure that you expected me to say that. If you did complete all the exercises, I congratulate you once again. If not, I urge you to complete the exercises at the end of each chapter.

You have a made a significant investment by this reading and taking appropriate action will ensure that you achieve the right ROI. Our partnership's goal was to create your success story, and I hope to have shown you some insights and tools that you can apply right away. Ours is a long-distance relationship and I can only ask you to live up to your promise and take necessary action starting today.

Find a partner

Implementation done alone is difficult and demands a large amount of discipline and commitment. I am not suggesting that you don't have them; however, I have observed time and again that people—despite with the right intentions and the right commitment and right discipline—fail to follow through. You need the help of a coach or a trusted partner who will hold you accountable for your plans and action items.

If you already have identified one and are working with him or her, congratulations! If you have not, it is extremely important that you identify one immediately.

When you are identifying your partner, find someone other than your family member or your close friends. They won't be objective a lot of times, and you can actually convince them with your excuses or superior logic, about not doing an exercise the way you were supposed to do it.

Share with someone

I had an opportunity to teach classes while I was studying, where I observed that what I had to teach were more interesting to me, and the concepts became a lot clearer. The fact that I had to be ready for questions made me prepare well, and research deeply.

When you review this book once again, do it with an intention of teaching some of the principles outlined here to someone else. You will notice that you will read the book with a different mindset when your intention is to teach.

Interact

I did tell you that you and I are in a partnership until you finish reading the book. I don't believe in short-term relationships. I am offering to extend our relationship for the future. Here are some ways that you can interact with me:

Newsletter: I am putting together a newsletter with some insights that I could reach to you via email. Your email address is never sold. You can find instructions to sign up for the newsletter at the companion website www.lifebeyondcode.com.

Send comments: You can send me comments about the book and your experiences about using the concepts from this book. We all thrive on feedback, and I would love to hear from you.

Success stories: Our goal in this partnership was to create your success story. I would be delighted to hear your success story, even if I played only a small part in it. Let me know if we can share your success story on the website.

Contribute: What is in this book is a compilation of what I have learned over the years. It includes lessons from my experience and from experiences of some of the finest consultants that I was fortunate to meet and work with. Do you have something that you think is worth sharing, and can be included in the future editions of the book? Drop me a quick note with whatever you want to share.

Meet: I speak at several events and my newsletters will include some of the events that I would be attending and/or speaking at. I would be happy to meet with you and discuss your questions at these sessions.

Blog: The companion website has a link to my blog, where I continue to write on topics discussed in this book. Feel welcome to participate in the discussions.

ACKNOWLEDGMENTS

Kavitha and Sumukh: For your patience and belief in me.

My parents and brother: For enduring my all my quirks, and for all your support without question.

Munwar, Manish, Harish & Amit: Co-founders of Cignex. In 2000, you believed in me, and we bootstrapped CIGNEX. I thank you all for your unwavering trust and friendship. You mean a lot to me.

Kannan Ayyar, Sterling Lanier, Yakov Soloveychik, Gary Hamel, Tim Sanders, Alok Khare, Seth Godin, Michael Weissman, Greg Winston, Dick Andreini, Steve Shapiro, Andy Fenselau, Bill Morton : My gurus and mentors. I am honored to be associated with you.

Tom Peters for writing the foreword for this book.

Mitesh Ashar: You brought me to Silicon Valley in 1997 when I didn't know what the Valley was. That changed my life completely, and I am indebted to you for that.

Karthik Sundaram: You were more than an editor. Apart from editing this work, you have challenged me along the way (rightly so), and made me think (again). Thank you for everything.

The TEC53 Group: For all the knowlegde and experiences we have all shared. Thanks, much!

Bill Sherman and **Joseph Mathai**: For all your inputs in shaping this book.

Don Moyer: You have been kind in donating one of your masterpieces to be reprinted in this book.

Kathryn Colletto and **Gaelen O'Connell**: The mindmaps you created for this book at Mindjet are simply amazing. Thanks!

Bill Gladstone, my agent, for moving at the speed of light.

Sarah Torrez, **Darius Miranda** and **Patrick Burns** for modeling the cover picture.

RECOMMENDED BOOKS

None of the authors referenced below have paid me to feature their books. They don't have to. They are here for a reason—these books are some of my favorites. I have made significant changes in my life after reading them, or I have seen someone close to me change positively as a result of reading these.

1. Seven Habits of Highly Effective People by *Stephen R Covey*

Why you should read it: Everyone knows the need to be proactive. Covey's book treats that subject with amazing flow. I treat this book as an all-time favorite and keep revisiting it often.

2. Influence by *Robert Cialdini*

Why you should read it: Great leaders are also great influencers You can learn the art of influencing if you read and apply the principles outlined in this book. The insights that I got from this book changed the way I deal with people—especially in sales situations.

3. Love is the Killer App by *Tim Sanders*

Why you should read it: Sanders clearly explains the importance of knowledge (why you should read more), network (how you should leverage your network) and compassion (dealing with people). Since I read that book I have made more than a hundred new connections between the people in my network without expecting a personal gain. It has worked great so far!

4. The Innovation Paradox by *Richard Farson*

Why you should read it: This is a very small book and a quick read, but it has taught me some of the biggest lessons in my life. Read this and you will start looking at both your successes and failures in a different light. You owe it to yourself!

5. Re-Imagine by *Tom Peters*

Why you should read it: Tom Peters is one of my heroes and I think *Re-Imagine* is one of his best works after *In Search of Excellence*. Peters reveals what has changed in business after 9/11, and how things are never going to be the same in the future, and how you can prepare for what's coming.

6. Leading the Revolution by *Gary Hamel*

Why you should read it: I have met Hamel numerous times, and I am always amazed by what he has to offer. His insights on innovation are fascinating, to say the least. The book covers more than innovation and deals with creating new business concepts in a systemic fashion.

7. The Fifth Discipline by *Peter Senge*

Why you should read it: When it comes to systems thinking, Peter Senge is the best. Every consultant should know about systems thinking, and I guess it is the first step towards learning the art of looking at the big picture.

8. Purple Cow by *Seth Godin*

Why you should read it: *Purple Cow* talks about creating remarkable companies. This book aims to transform you to be remarkable. Many concepts that Godin teaches in *Purple Cow* can be applied (with some changes) to yourself as a person.

9. Managing the Professional Services Firm by *David Maister*

Why you should read it: This is the best book on professional services. While the book is organized about managing a company, there is a ton of information that is useful to a consultant as well.

10. Unstoppable by *Cynthia Kersey*

Why you should read it: We all go through troubles and problems in life. Read this book and see how people have overcome obstacles to emerge as winners. These are real life stories and not figments of imagination—people like you and me displaying courage, commitment and tenacity to shape their lives.

11. NLP Business Masterclass by *David Molden*

Why you should read it: There are a number of great books on Neuro Linguistic Programming, but very few that treat the subject from a business context. Molden does a great job of blending NLP and business.

12. The Mind Map Book by *Tony Buzan*

Why you should read it: Learn the art of mind mapping from the creator of the concept. This got me started with mindmapping in 1993, and I use it even today for my life and my business. It's a great introduction to mindmapping.

clik 4 ram @ gahoo.com